Qualitative Methods in Social Work Research

SAGE SOURCEBOOKS FOR THE HUMAN SERVICES SERIES

Series Editors: ARMAND LAUFFER and CHARLES GARVIN

Recent Volumes in This Series

Qualitative Methods in Social Work Research

Challenges and Rewards

Sage Sourcebooks for

the Human Services
36

Deborah K. Padgett

SAGE Publications
International Educational and Professional Publisher
Thousand Oaks   London   New Delhi

For information:

SAGE Publications, Inc.
2455 Teller Road
Thousand Oaks, California 91320
E-mail: order@sagepub.com

SAGE Publications Ltd.
6 Bonhill Street
London EC2A 4PU
United Kingdom

SAGE Publications India Pvt. Ltd.
M-32 Market
Greater Kailash I
New Delhi 110 048 India

Printed in the United States of America

Library of Congress Cataloging-in-Publication Data
Padgett, Deborah K.
    Qualitative methods in social work research: Challenges and rewards/
by Deborah K. Padgett.
        p.   cm.—(Sage sourcebooks for the human services series; v. 36)
    Includes bibliographical references and index.
    ISBN 0-7619-0200-7 (cloth: acid-free paper)
    ISBN 0-7619-0201-5 (pbk.: acid-free paper)
        1. Social service—Research—Methodology. I. Title. II. Series.
    HV11.P24   1998
    361.3′ 072—dc21   97-33908

        00 01 02 03 04 10 9 8 7 6 5 4 3

Acquiring Editor:	Jim Nageotte
Editorial Assistant:	Fiona Lyons
Production Editor:	Astrid Virding
Production Assistant:	Karen Wiley
Typesetter/Designer:	Marion Warren
Indexer:	Teri Greenberg
Cover Designer:	Ravi Balasuriya
Print Buyer:	Anna Chin

CONTENTS

PREFACE

Because you have chosen to peruse this book, I am assuming that you have chosen to enter the world of qualitative research methods. Welcome. Qualitative methods are rapidly gaining ground as a viable approach for social workers and other researchers in clinically applied fields such as nursing, education, law, and medicine. Unlike training in quantitative methods and statistics, the choice of qualitative methods is still elective— no one *has* to learn how to conduct qualitative research.

Perhaps you are a doctoral student in social work considering your dissertation topic or an interested academic or agency-based researcher. This book is designed to start you on a journey of discovery. Of course, you may ultimately decide that qualitative methods are not for you. In either case, I hope that you will have learned about the various methods known as *qualitative* and made an informed decision.

BACKGROUND TO THIS BOOK

This book has its origins in the growing enthusiasm for qualitative methods in social work in recent years. However, the audience for this book is not necessarily confined to social work researchers. Although social work-related examples are offered, the chapters take an ecumenical approach and can be useful to a variety of practitioners and researchers in applied fields. I have reserved the Epilogue for discussion of specific issues surrounding inclusion of qualitative methods in social work education.

In the reflexive spirit of qualitative inquiry, it seems only fitting that I disclose a bit about my background and orientation. This book represents a return "home" for me, transversing paradigms along the way. Trained as a cultural anthropologist in the 1970s, I carried out "traditional" ethnographic fieldwork in a Serbian American community in Wisconsin and earned a doctorate in cultural anthropology. Wishing to focus more on mental health research, I completed a postdoctoral fellowship in quantitative methods and sociomedical sciences in 1986 at Columbia University's School of Public Health. This produced a career trajectory almost exclusively engaged in quantitative methods during the late 1980s and early 1990s.

After joining the faculty of New York University School of Social Work in 1988, becoming a social work researcher came naturally because my concerns with ethnicity, mental health, and services for the underserved dovetailed with those of my colleagues. Soon thereafter, I became aware of the growing popularity of qualitative methods in social work education, particularly in doctoral programs. Concurrently, I was seeing questions emerge from my quantitative research that could only be answered by more intensive inquiry.

During the early 1990s, I began collaborating with colleagues in qualitative sociology and community psychology in gaining funding from the National Cancer Institute to conduct a study of African American women and mammography, a quantitative study with a significant qualitative component. My return to qualitative methods in the Mammogram Study provided me with inspiration as well as concrete examples that are used in this book.

Jerome Bruner is credited with making the useful distinction between *training* and *educating* students, saying we do the former when we know what we're doing and the latter when we don't know what we're doing (cited in Wolcott, 1994, p. 392). Learning about qualitative methods entails a true process of education—it provides a window to the social sciences and humanities and provokes conceptual, critical, and creative thinking. Because it is taught by those of us who "don't know what we're doing," there are always opportunities to learn from students and from others' experiences. Learning and doing qualitative methods has been a source of deep satisfaction and lifelong discovery for me.

SCOPE AND ORGANIZATION
OF THE BOOK

This book places more emphasis on the "how-to" than the "what-is" aspects of qualitative methodology. But it is intended to be more of a conversation than a cookbook (because there is no single prescriptive recipe for doing qualitative research anyway). In writing this book, I drew on the experiences and cautionary tales of a number of qualitative researchers including myself. The emphasis is on pragmatism and flexibility.

As the reader will see in Chapter 1 and elsewhere, the term *qualitative methods* embraces a wide diversity of techniques and approaches. These diverse approaches coexist as a loosely connected family—a bit dysfunctional at times, but always interesting and lively.

This book presents chapters organized in a sequence of stages associated with carrying out qualitative methods. At the same time, the reader is cautioned that qualitative research is by no means a linear process. Instead, the qualitative researcher is engaged in a recursive zig-zag process for which there is no single recipe for guidance.

Chapter 1 gives a brief history of the theoretical and disciplinary origins of qualitative methods, grounds the reader in the language and terminology of qualitative research, and sets the stage for the "how-to" chapters that follow. It also offers a discussion of the similarities and differences between qualitative research and social work practice. Chapter 2 highlights one of the most salient (and salutary) aspects of qualitative methods—the role of the researcher as instrument of data collection. It is difficult to overestimate how critical this role is to the success of a qualitative study.

Chapters 3 through 7 take the reader through the various stages of carrying out qualitative research: selecting a topic and designing the study (Chapter 3), addressing ethical issues (Chapter 4), entering the field and sampling (Chapter 5), data collection (Chapter 6), and data analysis (Chapter 7). Chapter 8 is devoted to rigor in qualitative research, addressing what is often considered the Achilles heel of qualitative methods. Chapter 9 provides guidelines for "telling the story." Given the considerable latitude afforded qualitative researchers approaching the write-up phase, this chapter discusses ways to fuse creativity with scholarship to produce a report that is informative and readable in the best tradition of qualitative research.

Chapter 10 is devoted to multimethod studies—those that combine qualitative and quantitative methods either sequentially or concurrently.

Finally, the Epilogue presents a few suggestions for individuals considering qualitative research and for schools of social work that seek to include qualitative methods in their research infrastructures.

A few general points about the format and writing style of this book. First, I have tried to incorporate sensitivity to gender, culture, and other identity issues throughout the text. These sensitivities are necessary for ethical reasons to ensure respect for diversity. But they are also critical dimensions in qualitative research because of the closeness of the relationship between researcher and researched. Second, the awkwardness of nonsexist language usage has led me to alternate use of masculine and feminine pronouns in the text, to occasionally fall back on the *he/she* formulation, and to use plural pronouns on other occasions. I hope that this is not disconcerting to the reader.

The reader has probably already noted my liberal use of the first person. This more informal style of writing has become commonplace in qualitative methods texts (see e.g., Ely et al., 1991; Van Maanen, 1988; and Wolcott, 1990). It is a natural consequence of the trend toward informal relationships and self-disclosure in qualitative methods. I hope that this style makes reading about qualitative methods more interesting for you, the reader. It certainly made writing about qualitative methods more appealing for me. After years wrapped in the straitjacket writing style imposed on quantitative reports, I am pleased to be able to write more informally and playfully. By the same token, I have tried to avoid unnecessary jargon. Although I try to be erudite at all times (a state I achieve with sporadic success), I am also a firm believer in using plain language whenever possible.

This book is presented as a general introductory text to complement more specialized works in qualitative inquiry and to accompany coursework in qualitative methods. Once one goes beyond a general "how-to" text such as this, published works on qualitative research tend to be specialized either topically (e.g., books on use of computer software, on data analysis techniques, how to write up a qualitative study, etc.) or by substantive area (grounded theory, narrative studies, phenomenological inquiry, feminist theory, postmodern critique, etc.). I included citations for many of these works throughout the text that can be found in the References.

Most students find reading about qualitative research a refreshing break from the usual research texts. With few exceptions, the "world" of qualitative research is accessible and welcoming. Even more satisfying to read are the products of qualitative research—monographs, books, and articles describing the results of in-depth inquiry into the lives and experiences of respondents. A list of suggested monographs is provided at the end of Chapter 9.

When all is said and done, textbooks and coursework are not sufficient to provide expertise in qualitative methods—it also must be gained by actual experience in the "field." With this in mind, I invite you on a journey of discovery that I hope will keep you engaged and informed.

ACKNOWLEDGMENTS

As with any book, acknowledgments and gratitude are in order. First, I would like thank my colleagues Dr. Michael Yedidia, Dr. Carla Mariano, Dr. Denise Burnette, and Dr. Mark Fraser for sharing their ideas, course syllabi, and reading lists with me. I would also like to thank Dr. Kathy Ell, formerly Director of the Institute for the Advancement of Social Work Research and a professor at the University of Southern California School of Social Work, for urging me to conduct a workshop on qualitative methods for social workers (with financial support from IASWR and the National Institute of Mental Health).

I am deeply grateful to the African American women who participated in the Mammogram Study. As well, I thank my colleagues on the study, Michael Yedidia, Jon Kerner, Jeanne Mandelblatt, Dana-ain Davis, and Janette Walker, for sharing their expertise with me. My references to the Mammogram Study throughout this book are made possible by their effort and collaboration.

I am also grateful to the doctoral students in my qualitative methods seminar for providing me with challenges and encouragement as well as ideas about how qualitative methods and clinical social work can be made to fit together. Last but not least, I wish to thank my husband Paul Chudy for preparing the tables and figures in this book. His superb expertise in computer graphics was matched only by his enthusiastic support for this book.

Chapter 1

INTRODUCTION

WHAT DO WE MEAN
BY QUALITATIVE METHODS?

A colleague once astutely remarked that virtually anyone can read and understand qualitative research, whereas it takes a good deal of training and experience to successfully conduct qualitative research. It looks deceptively easy to do. In my experience, carrying out qualitative research is more labor intensive and demanding than carrying out quantitative methods. One cannot fall back on scientific method "recipes" to guide the process of inquiry—creativity and effort are required of the researcher.

For all of their demands, qualitative methods can provide the most rewarding experience a researcher will have. Their pursuit is akin to a voyage of discovery with all of the risks and rewards such a voyage entails. One can encounter stormy seas (angry informants or a disapproving thesis advisor) as well as smooth sailing (intense and exhilarating interviews and engagement on a fascinating topic). Or one can get stuck, becalmed in windless seas and unable to move on. Qualitative research takes constant vigilance, but the rewards of a successful voyage make it all worthwhile.

What exactly is meant by the term *qualitative methods*? There is no "one size fits all" qualitative method to make the definitional task easier. Indeed, qualitative research is best referred to as a family of methods, among whom some members are more compatible than others (Denzin & Lincoln, 1994; Riessman, 1994). The array of terms used to refer to this family of methods—ethnography, grounded theory, narrative analysis, constructivism, phenomenology, cultural studies, postmodernism, and so forth—only adds to the confusion. There is little standardization of terminology nor is such standardization necessarily desirable. In this book, I will use the phrase *qualitative methods,* occasionally substituting *naturalistic inquiry,* to refer to the basic qualitative research strategies—the common denominator that cuts across most of the family of methods.

Just as definitional clarity is missing within the qualitative methods family, the boundary between quantitative and qualitative methods is not clear. The tendency to dichotomize—"a mile wide and an inch deep" versus "a mile deep and an inch wide"—is misleading. Typically, quantitative studies are characterized by the use of numerical data and qualitative studies are distinguished by the use of nonnumeric textual data. But many researchers routinely transform qualitative data into numerical data. They may, for example, report counts and frequencies of events or behaviors as well as the demographic characteristics of their sample. Qualitative data categories may also be incorporated into statistical analyses of categoric data such as ANOVA (analysis of variance) or loglinear analyses. This capacity to transform qualitative data into numeric data affords a degree of choice and flexibility in writing up the findings of a study not available to quantitative researchers (because their data cannot be converted into true qualitative data).

The phrase *qualitative methods* implies more than the logistics of how data are collected and analyzed. To varying degrees, qualitative methods entail paradigmatic assumptions and approaches that set them apart from quantitative research in the natural and social sciences. These assumptions and approaches are summarized in Table 1.1.

Qualitative methods are inherently *inductive*; they seek to discover, not test, explanatory theories. They are *naturalistic,* favoring *in vivo* observation and interviewing of respondents over the decontextualizing approach of scientific inquiry. As such, they imply a degree of *closeness* and an *absence of controlled conditions* that stand in contrast to the distance and control of scientific studies. According to Manicas and Secord (1982), qualitative research is predicated on an "open systems" assumption where the observational context (and the observer) are part of the study itself. In contrast, quantitative research favors a "closed system" approach where every effort is made to neutralize the effects of the observational context (including the observer).

Qualitative studies seek to convey the complex worlds of respondents in an *holistic* manner using "thick description" rather than particularistic categories and variables. Furthermore, they assume a *dynamic reality,* a

Table 1.1

Distinctions Between Qualitative and Quantitative Research

Qualitative	*Quantitative*
Inductive	Deductive
Naturalistic; in vivo	Scientific Method
	Decontextualizing
Uncontrolled Conditions	Controlled Conditions
Open Systems	Closed Systems
Holistic; Thick Description	Particularistic
Dynamic Reality	Stable Reality
Researcher as Instrument	Standardized Data
of Data Collection	Collection Instruments
Categories Result from Data Analysis	Categories Precede Data Analysis

state of flux that can only be captured via prolonged engagement with respondents. Whereas the "heart" of a quantitative report is its statistical findings, a qualitative report is a *bricolage*, a pieced-together, tightly woven whole greater than the sum of its parts.

Doing qualitative research requires an unparalleled degree of immersion by the *researcher as the instrument of data collection.* Unlike the precoded standardized questionnaire, the qualitative researcher must be a sensitive instrument of observation, capable of developing categories of meaning from raw data.

It is helpful to think of members of the qualitative family as positioned along a continuum of accommodation with (or in opposition to) positivism and traditional scientific inquiry. Although it is difficult to know what proportion of qualitative researchers subscribe to a "rejectionist" point of view, I suspect that most (myself included) feel comfortable situated closer to the middle of the continuum. Here, qualitative researchers advocate a "many ways of knowing" approach that embraces multiple paradigms and methodologies (Berlin, 1990; Fraser, Taylor, Jackson, & O'Jack, 1991; Hartman, 1994; Proctor, 1990).

There are similarities between quantitative and qualitative methods that are too often overlooked. First, both approaches are *empirical,* relying on first-hand observation and data collection to guide findings and conclusions. Charles Darwin and Alfred Russel Wallace both proposed a theory of evolution at the same time, but only Darwin backed up his argument with intensive observation in the Galapagos Islands and elsewhere during his 5-year voyage on the *Beagle.* By comparison, Wallace was an armchair thinker, relying on data gathered by others.

Both types of empirical data—qualitative or quantitative—may be used in scientific inquiry. Neither type of data is inherently "scientific" or "nonscientific." The difference lies in the greater likelihood that qualitative researchers will deploy interpretive paradigms that are not hypothetico-deductive as prescribed by the scientific method.

Second, both qualitative and quantitative methods are *systematic.* Contrary to a popular misperception, qualitative research is neither haphazard nor unfocused. Yet, systematic research need not be prescriptive and rigidly predictable. It can also be flexible.

Students new to qualitative research invariably ask the "how many" questions: How many respondents will I need in my sample? How many interviews are needed? How many months should I spend in the field? How many questions should I ask? How many pages of transcripts are enough? This need for answers early on is understandable because quantitative studies typically provide these answers. But these questions also reveal a lack of awareness of what qualitative research is about. Qualitative studies have an open-ended, unpredictable nature that mitigates against answering any of the "how many" questions with certainty and finality.

THEORETICAL AND DISCIPLINARY
ORIGINS OF QUALITATIVE METHODS

The scope and purpose of this book do not allow an in-depth treatment of the long and complex history of this methodology. Nevertheless, it is useful to provide an overview of the "donor disciplines" such as anthropology, sociology, philosophy, and linguistics (McCracken, 1988), as well as the "recipient disciplines" that have enthusiastically embraced and extended qualitative methods. The latter include (in rough chronological order): education, nursing, psychology and social work.

The longest tradition of qualitative inquiry belongs to anthropology, originating with late 19th-century ethnographies of non-Western peoples and cultures and continuing today, although in a different form. The era of the Lone Ethnographer (Rosaldo, 1989), which extended until World War II, introduced most of the defining characteristics of qualitative methods shown in Table 1.1. The contrast to a laboratory scientist working in a laboratory could not have been greater.

Interestingly, the leading anthropologists of the day—Boas, Kluckoln, Malinowski, Lowie, Benedict, Mead—offered little guidance in the "how-to" aspect of ethnographic fieldwork. This tradition of learning-by-doing continues today; curricula in most anthropology graduate programs offer little formal coursework in research methods.

By the end of World War II, the Chicago School of sociology had begun to produce a rich and varied body of qualitative research based on observations closer to home, including studies of medical schools (Becker, Geer, Hughes, & Strauss, 1961) and whole towns and communities (Lynd & Lynd, 1937, 1956). Based at the University of Chicago, the sociology department pioneered an approach that became systematized as a unique methodology, beginning with the early leadership of Robert Park, Ernest Burgess, and W. I. Thomas, and culminating with the publication of *The Discovery of Grounded Theory* by Glaser and Strauss (1967).

Although also inductive and holistic in approach, sociological qualitative research has been more concerned with theory building than its sister discipline of anthropology. Anthropologists have tended to honor "field labor"—excellence in idiographic description—over theory generation (Van Maanen, 1988).

A number of exemplary qualitative studies of American life were produced by sociologists and anthropologists during this "golden era" extending into the 1960s, including Whyte's *Street Corner Society* (1955), Goffman's *Asylums* (1961), Powdermaker's *Stranger and Friend* (1966), Liebow's *Talley's Corner* (1967), and Stack's *All Our Kin* (1974). These works endure as classic examples of *verstehen*—understanding the ways of others via participant observation.

The codification and documentation of qualitative methodology during the 1970s and 1980s were heavily influenced by Glaser and Strauss's (1967) grounded theory approach, but also by the works of anthropologically trained researchers in educational evaluation such as George and Louise Spindler, Jules Henry, and Harry Wolcott. The value of qualitative methods for educational evaluation is further manifested in the valuable works of Yvonna Lincoln and Egon Guba (Guba, 1990; Guba & Lincoln, 1981, 1989; Lincoln & Guba, 1985), Bogdan and Taylor (1975, 1994), and Taylor and Bogdan (1984).

By the mid-1970s, a more reflexively critical paradigm began to emerge within qualitative research that questioned the Cartesian assumptions of positivism and "value-free" scientific inquiry. Although the intellectual underpinnings of this movement can be traced to European philosophers (such as Kant, Dilthey, and Wittgenstein) and to French deconstructionism inspired by Jacques Derrida and others, its impetus came from 1960s activism and dissatisfaction with the status quo. Heavily influenced by the writings of anthropologist Clifford Geertz (1973, 1983), its proponents argued that traditional ethnography was not a privileged search for Truth, but was deeply embedded in the Eurocentric biases of the colonial and postcolonial eras. A new perspective emerged from this critique, one that emphasized reflexivity and introspection, immersion in thick description of specific locales, and pluralistic standpoints. This scenario fit well with Kuhn's (1970) depiction of the sudden displacement of scientific theories that are delegitimized by more powerful explanatory models, or paradigms.

This "crisis of representation" (Denzin & Lincoln, 1994) inspired a good deal of soul searching in anthropology (Atkinson, 1990; Clifford & Marcus, 1986; Rabinow & Sullivan, 1979) and a new form of ethnography emerged. In traditional ethnographic reports, the observer was missing from the report, yet spoke in an omniscient voice in describing the Other. In the new ethnography, the observer became a central figure in the drama of fieldwork, a flesh-and-blood human being absolved of any claims to scientific authority.

Many anthropologists and sociologists in the 1980s identified with the postmodern movement then transforming academic and intellectual circles in the United States and Western Europe. Disciplinary boundaries became blurred as social scientists embraced the approaches of the humanities— philosophy, literature, the arts—and produced works that no longer resembled scientific reports. Instead, they wrote memoirs, essays, and theoretical or conceptual treatises. Norman Denzin (1978) in sociology and Guba and Lincoln (1985) in education led the way in defining a naturalistic *constructionist* perspective compatible with postmodern sensibilities. The *Handbook of Qualitative Research* (Denzin & Lincoln, 1994) represents a compendium of works in the constructionist tradition.

This picture of intellectual ferment would not be complete without mentioning the feminist theorists who criticized the scientific paradigm as male biased and logocentric (Harding, 1986; Reinharz, 1992). Many feminist and postmodern critics joined forces in opposing a common foe, arguing that there is no one Truth to be discovered by an impartial (presumably male) scientist, but many truths awaiting discovery.

Of course, not all qualitative researchers subscribe to the postmodernist approach. Sociologists John and Lyn Lofland (1995) argued that the more useful insights of postmodernism are largely "old wine in new bottles"

(p. xvii) and that elements of the movement reveal a "nihilistic and sophistic" (p. xvii) bent. Countering the postmodernist depiction of science as unfairly distorted, the Loflands contended that positivist scientists do not lay claims to discovering the Truth and willingly accept that knowledge is socially constructed and provisional. In short, they did not agree with the notion that all information is interpretation.

Clearly, the logic of postmodernism and cultural relativism can be taken to an extreme; the "many realities" approach becomes a hall of mirrors where all knowledge is suspect. In this context, we can never verify how many died in the Nazi Holocaust or in the Serbian massacres in Bosnia in the 1990s because these horrific incidents can be seen via many interpretive standpoints—none privileged. This statement may seem far-fetched but it follows a line of reasoning consistent with postmodern assertions regarding the fictitiousness of facts (Lofland & Lofland, 1995).

The field of social work has not remained immune to the attractions of postmodernism (Chambon & Irving, 1994). But I believe that the Loflands' critique holds special relevance for social work. The arid detachment of the postmodern movement appears inappropriate and potentially harmful amid the crises in social and health-care services that beset the poor and vulnerable.

REASONS FOR DOING QUALITATIVE RESEARCH

What kinds of research objectives might lead you to choose qualitative research? There are several scenarios possible. These are not mutually exclusive, nor are they exhaustive. But they do provide some of the more common pathways to becoming a qualitative researcher.

1. *You want to explore a topic about which little is known.* This approach conforms to an enduring assumption about qualitative methods—they work best during the initial exploratory phase of inquiry (after which "hard" science takes over). There are many topics that place us at a frontier of sorts—the experiences of grandmothers caring for grandchildren orphaned by AIDS, domestic abuse among gays and lesbians, the identity of interracial children amid changing definitions of race and ethnicity, the experience of menopause by women taking hormone-replacement therapy drugs, parenting adopted children from foreign countries who suffered from emotional and physical abuse, posttraumatic stress syndrome among female adolescents victimized by

violence and abuse, coping by single fathers with sole custody, decision making about abortion by pregnant teenage girls, grieving the loss of a family member to assisted suicide, and so forth. Such topics need not be pristinely untouched. What is important is that too little is known about them and an in-depth understanding is desired.

2. *You are pursuing a topic of sensitivity and emotional depth.* Social workers encounter on a daily basis human crises and dilemmas that require empathy and understanding. These professional experiences, in turn, provide a wellspring of ideas for research. For many of these topics, the use of a standardized, close-ended interview would be inappropriate or insensitive. If, for example, you are interested in incest survivors, you would probably not find out much via a questionnaire.

For researchers interested in behaviors considered taboo by society, qualitative methods may be the only approach plausible. Ethnographic studies of heroin addicts, gang members, sex workers, car thieves, and transvestites portray the lives of individuals who are not likely to cooperate with the usual forms of survey research. Moreover, studies of the taboo need not be confined to the fringes of polite society—one can "study up" as well as "study down." Whether from the worlds of business, the professions, or politics, members of an elite target population are often the hardest to study. Because they are powerful, they can limit access and fend off the overtures of a researcher in ways that the poor cannot (Hertz & Imber, 1995). They may also fear they have much to lose by cooperating with a qualitative interviewer.

3. *You wish to capture the "lived experience" from the perspectives of those who live it and create meaning from it.* When the researcher seeks *verstehen,* or understanding, qualitative methods are invariably the path to take. Such studies are *emic,* capturing the respondent's point of view, rather than *etic,* seeking to explain from the perspective of an "objective" outsider.

The emic versus etic distinction originated some time ago in anthropology (Harris, 1968), reflecting the adaptation of linguistic terminology (phonemic vs. phonetic) to describe how the ethnographer's role has evolved away from a "scientist of culture" to a portrayer of meaning-in-context (Schwandt, 1994). As such, it is a useful heuristic device embraced by many qualitative researchers.

There are times when we seek *verstehen,* whether we are exploring the life course of an elderly homeless woman, the experiences of chronic pain patients, or ethical dilemmas of caseworkers in a child welfare agency. The ways in which respondents view their worlds and create meaning from diverse life experiences are myriad and can best be tapped by a qualitative approach.

4. *You wish to get inside the "black box" of programs and interventions.* Program and practice evaluation typically distinguish between *process* (what takes place during the intervention) and *outcome* (success or failure in achieving the program's goals). Given inevitable constraints of time and resources, the emphasis in program evaluation has been more on operationalizing and measuring outcomes than on process (Dehar, Casswell, & Duignan, 1993). Qualitative methods have proven useful for studies of outcome (Huberman & Miles, 1994; Levine & Zimmerman, 1996).

Qualitative program evaluation has a long and honorable history in the field of education (Bogdan & Taylor, 1994; Cook & Reichart, 1979; Fetterman, 1989; Guba & Lincoln, 1981, 1989; Patton, 1990; Scriven, 1967; Stake, 1975). Social work researchers have also used qualitative approaches to evaluate programs in mental health services (Everett & Boydell, 1994; Grigsby, 1992; Pulice, 1994; Pulice, McCormick, & Dewees, 1995; Weinberg & Koegel, 1996), home-based family treatment (Fraser & Haapala, 1987) and child welfare (Rodwell & Woody, 1994).

Qualitative methods excel when used to explore the inner workings of the black box—the *process* dimension of program evaluation (see Figure 1.1). They complement the quantitative findings by providing more in-depth understanding of how the experimental intervention succeeded (or failed). Even rigorously "manualized" therapies such as cognitive behavioral treatment for depression leave open the possibility that subtle differences in their implementation may produce individual variation in treatment response (Drake et al., 1993).

5. *You are a quantitative researcher who has reached an impasse in data collection or in explaining findings.* In speaking with research colleagues, I am struck by how often questions emerge during quantitative studies that cry out for qualitative research. This can happen in the midst of data collection or after the findings are in.

At times, a quantitative study is fine as far as it goes, but the findings cannot be explained without resorting to qualitative inquiry. My quantitative research on ethnic differences in mental health help-seeking has frequently led me to fall back on the "cultural" explanation and a call for more in-depth studies of how members of ethnic minority groups perceive mental illness and the mental health delivery system (Padgett, Patrick, Burns, & Schlesinger, 1994).

BASELINE DATA

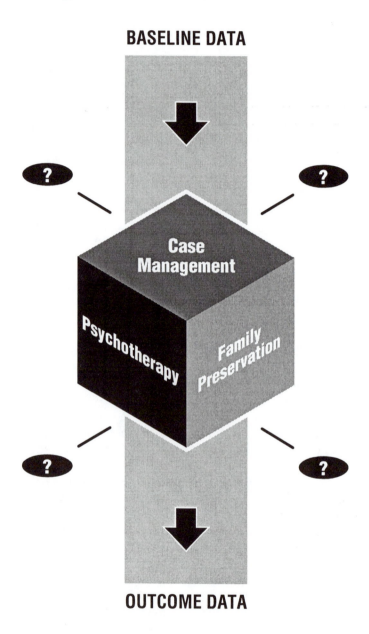

OUTCOME DATA

Figure 1.1. The Black Box

6. *You are seeking to merge activism with research. Action,* or *participatory, research* is devoted to fighting oppression and social injustice (Cancian, 1993; Fals-Borda & Rahman, 1991; Reason, 1994; Reinharz, 1992; Stringer, 1996). Rooted in the efforts of community activists, feminists, and Third World liberation movements of the 1960s and 1970s, action research seeks to fuse knowledge building with empowerment and social advocacy (Cancian, 1993). In action research, those who are studied—members of oppressed groups—maintain substantial control over the study from start to finish (Cancian, 1993).

Both qualitative and quantitative methods can be (and have been) used to pursue activist goals, but the central premises of action research more closely fit the relationship of the researcher and the researched in qualitative studies. Yet, the vast majority of studies in social work (and in qualitative research in general) do not follow the action model. Why? The marriage of action and research *throughout the course of the study* requires some discomfiting tradeoffs, most prominently the erosion of rigor that comes with the loss of critical distance and loss of control over the study's methods.

In summary, there are many sound reasons to do qualitative research. There are also very good reasons *not* to do qualitative research. If you are looking for an easy way to carry out interesting research, be forewarned. The degree of labor intensity—drawing on the researcher's time and emotional resources—is unmatched by any other form of inquiry. Second, if you feel you do not come close to fitting the profile of traits and skills outlined in the next chapter, you should think twice about going further. Last, if you are concerned with scientific utility and with procuring research funding from government or private foundations, proposing a qualitative study will probably reduce your chances of success. It is better to think of qualitative research as a labor of love than as the fast track to the researchers' hall of fame. The primary reason for doing qualitative research is the same as it ever was: the thirst for knowledge and understanding.

MYTHS ABOUT
QUALITATIVE RESEARCH

Despite their intuitive appeal to many researchers in a variety of fields, qualitative methods remain sorely misunderstood and denigrated by many in the scientific community. Scorned as "soft," or nonscientific, these methods have been deemed unworthy of serious researchers. They have been viewed as an unsystematic unfocused endeavor using small, nonrepresentative samples to produce impressionistic findings vulnerable to almost any bias one could imagine. This portrayal of qualitative research is probably more the product of ignorance than of malice. Nevertheless, these myths permeate the scientific community and hinder qualitative researchers when they seek funding, approval for doctoral dissertations, and publication in most academic journals.

At the other extreme, some zealous proponents have themselves contributed to the mythification of qualitative research. They portray qualitative methods in mystical terms, an approach to inquiry that requires creativity and special talents open only to a select few and their devoted followers (McCracken, 1988). Some of these "mythifiers" are probably motivated by the unfair marginalization of qualitative research by the scientific community. Others undoubtedly believe that the qualitative approach is superior to all others as a path to Enlightenment. However, by offering exaggerated claims, these proponents contribute to misunderstandings and undermine their own arguments in favor of qualitative research.

The lack of standardized norms for training qualitative researchers and for evaluating the quality of this methodology fuels misunderstanding and mystification. If there are diverse approaches with no consensus on evaluative criteria of quality, intellectual authority too often resides with those who are viewed as experts (or intellectual gurus). As expertise becomes personified, its acquisition depends on following the leader—a situation not very conducive to critical thinking (Gambrill, 1995). The idea that qualitative methods can only be learned at the feet of a master is, in my opinion, nonsense. These methods can be taught to all interested parties and can be conducted in a rigorous, accountable manner. Although the task is made more challenging by the absence of a single "gold standard" approach, it is far from daunting.

QUALITATIVE RESEARCH
AND SOCIAL WORK PRACTICE:
SIMILARITIES AND DIFFERENCES

In recent years, a growing number of doctoral programs in social work have eagerly embraced qualitative methods. The attraction of these methods for practitioners is powerful. At first glance, the parallels between qualitative research and clinical social work are striking, a "hand in glove" fit (Gilgun, 1994). Gilgun offered several examples of how social work practice resembles qualitative research. Thus, social workers start "where the client is," view clients as part of a wider social context, and favor individualized assessment and maximum detail in chronicling the lives of clients. Furthermore, they think inductively and flexibly, examining information from a variety of sources before drawing conclusions about a client's problems and appropriate treatment, and responding to new information by modifying treatment approaches.

The primary methods of data collection in qualitative research—in-depth interviewing, observation, and document review—are familiar to social workers. The basic record-keeping tasks of social work practice—process recording, memoing, and case reporting—are quite similar to the processes of data analysis used by qualitative researchers. The emphasis on naturalistic inquiry valued by qualitative researchers is familiar to social workers accustomed to visiting clients' homes and communities (Gilgun, 1994).

Of the various methods of data collection in research, qualitative interviewing in particular bears a strong resemblance to a therapeutic interview. The parallels are obvious: Both types of interviewing elicit thoughts, memories, and feelings in a "safe" nonjudgmental environment established by an empathic interviewer (Weiss, 1994). Both entail a joint search for meaning and understanding.

Yet, there are crucial differences between social work practice and qualitative research—differences that are ignored at the researcher's peril. Psychologist Edgar H. Schein (1987) and sociologist Robert S. Weiss (1994) provided helpful discussions of how the clinician differs from the qualitative researcher. Their observations, along with some of my own, form the basis of Table 1.2. The contrast here is based on the role occupied by the vast majority of social workers in agency and private practice, helping clients and their families overcome problems in their lives. A more detailed discussion of these issues can be found in Padgett (in press).

As shown in Table 1.2, the differences between the social work practitioner and the qualitative researcher span a number of key domains ranging from paradigm assumptions to the criteria for success. The *paradigmatic assumptions* of the practitioner assume a normative state of health; her role is to identify pathology and work to restore health. Although social workers are trained to employ a holistic, person-in-

Table 1.2

Contrasts Between Clinical Social Work Practice and Qualitative Research[*]

Domains	Clinical Practice	Qualitative Research
Paradigm assumptions	Theory and model driven Normative	Theory generation Non-normative
Goals	Clinical mandate Helping	Knowledge Scholarship
Education and training	Coursework Supervised practice	Coursework Little or no supervision in the field
Disciplinary influences	Social work Psychology Social sciences	Anthropology Sociology Humanities/philosophy
Client/respondent relationship	Initiated by client Problem solving Terminated by client improvement Time is scheduled "50 minute hour"	Initiated by researcher Non-clinical Terminated by researcher Time is unscheduled and prolonged
Criteria for success	Client improvement Recognition of peers Non-standardized criteria	Scholarship Rigor Recognition of peers Non-standardized criteria

[*]Contrasts in this table are based upon work by Schein (1987), Weiss (1994), and Padgett (in press). Reprinted with permission. Copyright 1998, National Association of Social Workers, Inc., *Social Work.*

environment perspective, their clinical theories are typically drawn from psychology, where individual problems are the target of concern.

In contrast, qualitative researchers seek to avoid normative assumptions and even go to great lengths to identify these as threats to the integrity of the study. Whereas preexisting theories may influence the study, the approach is one of theory generation and emergent (rather than preexisting) conceptual frameworks.

Divergence in *goals* distinguishes practitioners from qualitative researchers. Practitioners' ultimate responsibilities are to serve their clients. No such clinical mandate exists for qualitative researchers. Their ultimate responsibilities lie in contributing knowledge and understanding in the form of rigorous scholarship, not providing services to a client or to a community.

Education and training, as well as *disciplinary influences,* also differ for social work practitioners and qualitative researchers. Social workers' education and training draw on the unique configuration of field-based internships and coursework influenced by theories of human behavior. Although social work students may be exposed to social science theories, their exposure is reduced by the demands of a curriculum designed to train future practitioners.

Learning about and doing qualitative research entails an unprecedented degree of autonomy. Compared to social work practice where close supervision is required for a period of years before autonomous practice can be carried out, qualitative researchers who enter the field must rely on their own judgment much of the time. Although they may seek support from peers and teachers, the basic tasks of fieldwork are largely conducted alone.

In addition to legal ramifications of clinical work such as mandated reporting, a number of aspects of the practitioner-client relationship are distinct from the researcher-respondent relationship. As noted by Schein (1987), the clinical relationship is initiated by the client, and the clinician is paid by the client or by a third party. In contrast, the qualitative researcher initiates the relationship, selects the site and respondents, and receives no payments for her efforts. Unlike the clinical relationship where expertise and authority flow "downward" from the practitioner, the locus of power and authority lies with the respondents. The researcher enters the relationship to learn from them, not vice versa.

Not surprisingly, a clinical session differs considerably from a research interview. Unlike clinicians, researchers focus on events and experiences, not problems and emotions. The respondent is encouraged to share feelings only if he volunteers such information or if it is useful for the study, or both (Weiss, 1994). Moreover, it would be inappropriate to suggest clinical interpretations to respondents even if (or especially if) they seek such advice.

In clinical relationships, disclosure is for the most part a one-way street; self-disclosure by the clinician is potentially damaging to the relationship. In qualitative research, self-disclosure is not only acceptable, but at times desirable as a means of enhancing rapport. Of course, the researcher should never use self-disclosure to displace the respondent under the spotlight.

In the clinical relationship, the decision to terminate is made by the client, the clinician, or both, usually based on a decision that the client's status has sufficiently improved. In qualitative research, the relationship ends when the researcher has decided that enough information has been acquired (unless, of course, the respondent decides to withdraw from the study). Further, the researcher's job does not end when data collection and active engagement are over. As opposed to the clinician's role, the tasks of data reduction, analysis, and write-up mark the continuation and completion of the researcher role (Schein, 1987).

Even the element of time is viewed differently. The clinical relationship typically proceeds through a series of regularly scheduled "50-minute hours." By comparison, the researcher's time in the field is erratic, often unpredictable, and always prolonged. The length of an interview is largely determined by the respondents rather than the researcher—the researcher must go with the flow and relinquish control over how time is spent.

Finally, *criteria for success*—the sources of validation, credibility, and approval for a job well done—are different for clinicians and qualitative researchers. Clinicians gain satisfaction from seeing improvements in their clients' lives. Professional prestige further accrues from the recognition and approval of clinical peers. Although measurable outcomes are increasingly relied on for evaluating practice, clinical effectiveness is still largely a product of the perceptions of clinicians and their clients.

Qualitative researchers share with their clinical peers a lack of consensus on how to evaluate the success of their efforts. But the absence of agreed-on standards for validation does not mean that criteria for rigor are unimportant or unavailable (a topic to be explored further in Chapter 8). Whereas clinicians achieve success via client improvement and peer recognition, researchers' success lies in the production of rigorous, scholarly work.

The reader may have noticed by now that I have devoted more space to discussing the differences between qualitative research and clinical social work practice than to discussing their similiarities. This was done deliberately to address what I see as a misperception that qualitative research is virtually synonymous with clinical practice.

Yet, I must admit that the boundaries between clinical practice and qualitative research are blurry at times. Clinicians may become participant observers in their own agencies or their assessment techniques may resemble a qualitative interview. Similarly, qualitative researchers in the field often find themselves offering various types of assistance to their respondents and assuming a quasi-therapeutic stance by simply being a good listener. Nevertheless, role confusion for the practitioner who becomes a qualitative researcher should be avoided if at all possible.

SUMMARY AND CONCLUSION

A few themes emerge from this chapter:

1. The diverse "family" of qualitative methods originated with the pioneering ethnographers of late 19th-century anthropology. By the late 20th century, the family had grown into an array of approaches influenced by the social sciences and humanities.

2. Like quantitative methods, qualitative methods are *empirical* and *systematic*. However, qualitative methods share features in common that set them apart from quantitative methods. Although varied in epistemological stance (ranging from positivist to postmodern antipositivist), qualitative methods in general are *inductive* and *naturalistic*. They assume that studies take place in "open systems" within a dynamic (rather than static) reality. Finally, they involve a close relationship between the researcher (who is the instrument of data collection) and the researched.

3. Qualitative methods have been the subject of mythification by their detractors as well as by their more zealous proponents. Regrettably, the persistence of myths—both critical and laudatory—inhibits a true understanding of the qualitative approach.

4. Qualitative methods are not synonymous with social work practice. Indeed, there are several critical dimensions on which research and practice differ.

Chapter 2

THE RESEARCHER
AS INSTRUMENT

If qualitative research is a voyage of discovery, then the researcher is the captain and the navigator of the ship. It is difficult to underestimate the significance of this role. Paraphrasing the French anthropologist Claude Lévi-Strauss (1966), the qualitative researcher is a *bricoleur,* a Jack (or Jill) of all trades, a professional do-it-yourselfer who creates a *bricolage,* a pieced-together construction of ideas. We must be pragmatic and creative, deploying multiple methods and approaches to produce new knowledge in often unpredictable ways.

Qualitative research need not be conducted by a single investigator. As we will see in Chapter 10, the team approach can be very effective. But the "soup-to-nuts" aspect to carrying out qualitative studies, combined with the demands of flexibility and creativity, are difficult to juggle when more than one person is involved. As a result, the tradition of the Lone Investigator is still the rule rather than the exception. This is not to say that we work in a vacuum—advice and feedback from others is critical.

In the Epilogue of this book, I will argue that social work students should have the opportunity to learn about qualitative methods and be encouraged to embark on research careers based on qualitative methods. Of course, this approach does not fit everyone's needs and capabilities. The purpose of this chapter is to discuss those individual qualities most suited to the conduct of qualitative research. It is hoped that this discussion will help you to decide if qualitative research suits you.

The abilities needed to successfully carry out qualitative research draw on a number of talents, traits, and skills. The researcher's unique position as the instrument of data collection imposes special burdens as well as opportunities. By comparison, quantitative researchers rely on standardized questionnaires and measures. Assuming their instructions are followed carefully, they yield quantitative data that do not vary according to the abilities and personal qualities of the researcher. Quantitative research designs also provide a degree of structure that guides the process and reduces ambiguity and uncertainty.

A qualitative study's success depends much more on the researcher's personal qualities as well as intellectual capacity. The absence of structure allows wide latitude—to reach creative heights as well as the depths of intellectual paralysis. The researcher engages in rewarding relationships, but she can also become overinvolved and emotionally exhausted. In other words, the margin of excellence—and of error—is wide.

DESIRABLE CHARACTERISTICS OF THE QUALITATIVE RESEARCHER

There are a number of traits or skills that help make a good qualitative researcher. The following listing of these traits is by no means exhaustive or even mutually exclusive. If a single individual possesses all of these traits in abundance, he or she is ideally positioned to conduct qualitative research. Of course, such an event is rare in nature—these desirable qualities are possessed to varying degrees by many people.

First are the qualities of *creativity* and *scholarship* (Mariano, 1990). This harks back to the distinction between training and education. Training in auto repair (or heart valve replacement) is, of necessity, formulaic, as the goal is to produce trained specialists with a minimal margin of error. In contrast, qualitative research draws on creativity and original insights, giving the investigator broad discretion in pursuing research goals.

At the same time, the pursuit of qualitative research must also be anchored in scholarship. Although qualitative researchers may pick and choose among a wide array of conceptual, theoretical, and disciplinary approaches, they are obliged to ground themselves in the scholarly literature. The degree of immersion may vary from deep and wide (for a doctoral dissertation) to a narrower, focused approach (for a time-limited program evaluation). What is important is that the researcher identify with the scholarly enterprise.

Second, qualitative researchers need to possess *maturity* and *self-discipline*. Anyone who has difficulties maintaining a professional demeanor when faced with rejection, traumatic revelations, or excruciating boredom should think twice before embarking on qualitative studies. The need for self-discipline is constant, from the early phases of the study when it seems as if all of our potential respondents refuse our invitation to participate, to the final phases when the data are piled into boxes (or on computer diskettes) waiting to be analyzed.

Related to this, qualitative researchers need to be able to maintain *critical distance*. The credibility of a qualitative study depends on the researcher's ability to exercise restraint. No matter how overwhelming is our desire to fix things, we must resist the temptation. Similarly, no matter how repugnant our respondents appear to us, we must withhold judgment as much as humanly possible.

Emotion management is easier for doctors and other clinicians because they have the protective distance associated with professional authority. But the qualitative researcher's position is more akin to the emotional management dilemmas of flight attendants observed by qualitative sociologist Arlie Hochschild (1983). Thus, we must maintain professional poise and amiability even when we find ourselves in the most exasperating circumstances.

We also need to be *flexible* and *reflexive*. Flexibility is a state of mind and of behavior (Ely et al., 1991). Cognitive or theoretical rigidity can interfere with the ability to observe and appreciate differing perspectives. If you are an ardent proponent of a clinical or social science theory, you may be wearing intellectual blinders that hinder observation and analysis.

The unpredictable, ever-changing landscape of naturalistic inquiry also demands behavioral flexibility on the part of the researcher. We encounter situations that require improvisation and quick thinking. Respondents may suddenly refuse to cooperate, continuously put off being interviewed or simply not show up at the scheduled time. They may divulge shocking information or make sexual overtures. An angry spouse may interrupt an interview and demand that you leave. Or the school principal who gave you approval to conduct the study is suddenly fired from her job. These scenarios are not far-fetched—they are commonplace. Much of the strength and success of qualitative research lies in its emergent nature, its ability to "go with the flow" rather than control it. If you are more comfortable working within a structured environment, qualitative research is not for you.

Reflexivity, the ability to examine one's self, is a central preoccupation in qualitative research. As noted by Michael Agar (1980), "the problem is not whether the ethnographer is biased; the problem is what kinds of biases exist . . . and how can their operation be documented" (p. 42). Examining one's biases is not a one-time thing, but requires ongoing vigilance throughout the course of the study. By doing so, we do not seek to eliminate personal beliefs and biases, but to understand their impact on the study.

In addition to personal qualities, certain skills are essential to the qualitative research enterprise. Among these are the skills of *observation* and *interpersonal communication*. Both of these are common elements of the social work practitioner's training, but their application in qualitative research follows a different tack. For example, when teaching qualitative methods, I ask my students to carry out an exercise in participant observation. They must go to the public place of their choice (a park, subway station, street fair, playground, etc.), observe the action for 1 hour, and write up field notes describing what they have seen. What a departure this is for them! Trained to actively engage clients and focus on problem resolution, they must be passive observers of all they can see. The open-ended nature of qualitative observation can be awkward and even painful for individuals more comfortable with the "filters" of clinical or personal theories.

The interpersonal skills of *empathy* and *sensitivity,* so important in social work practice, are put to somewhat different ends in qualitative research. Rather than actively engage with clients to achieve treatment goals, we become listeners seeking knowledge and understanding. This requires a degree of humility and subordination of self that takes some getting used to.

As if the above were not enough, we must conclude with two of the most essential skills needed in qualitative research—the interrelated abilities to *think conceptually* and *write well.* The need to think abstractly and create new conceptual frameworks (rather than test existing concepts and theories as in deductive research) is the sine qua non of qualitative methods. Termed *theoretical sensitivity* by Glaser (1978), this attribute refers to the ability to give meaning to data, to separate the wheat from the chaff. Formulating ideas, developing concepts and theories that meaningfully capture some phenomenon, and being able to write both concisely and elegantly—these are traits that enable a qualitative researcher to go far.

Quantitative researchers also need to know how to think conceptually, but the success of their efforts does not hinge as much on having these capabilities. For example, a quantitative researcher can draw on an existing array of concepts and measures for the study's conceptual framework and even hire a statistician to carry out the data analyses. By comparison, analyzing qualitative data is more closely analogous to an artist sculpting than to a cook following a recipe.

A good sense of humor helps enormously in qualitative research, particularly the ability to laugh at oneself. Our vulnerability and inexperience when entering the field almost guarantee that we will make mistakes, and some of them will be funny in the eyes of others (anthropologists invariably have stories of abject humiliation and jokes made at their expense). If our blunders are funny to our respondents, we might as well laugh with them. The researcher who takes him- or herself too seriously can quickly get bogged down in the field.

Insider humor also has its place. During Charles Bosk's (1979) ethnographic study of hospital surgeons, he found their macabre humor off-putting at first, but then saw how these jokes helped to break the tension among housestaff. Similarly, Sue Estroff's (1981) immersion in the worlds of psychiatric outpatients exposed her to sexual ribaldry and "crazy" jokes that only an insider could appreciate.

THE IMPACT OF QUALITATIVE
RESEARCH ON THE RESEARCHER

Few of us complete a qualitative study without being changed in some way (Daniels, 1983). For good or ill, the depth and intensity of the experience leaves its mark on the researcher. The persons we learn from— AIDS patients, the homeless, the severely mentally ill, and the chronically ill—bring us into their worlds of pain as well as joy. We spend long periods of time with them—how could it be otherwise?

Often, our respondents hold up a mirror to us and challenge us. Barbara Myerhoff (1978), a social worker and anthropologist, wrote movingly about her experiences studying elderly Jewish women at a community center:

> Many of the Center people continued to "make" me feel guilty. After greeting me warmly, Basha would often ask, "Never mind these other things you all the time ask about. Tell me, who's with your children?" . . . When I was away too long, they scolded and snubbed me . . . My presence was a continual reminder of many painful facts: that it should have been their own children there listening to their stories; that I had combined family and a career, opportunities that the women had longed for and never been allowed. And too, that I knew so little of their background suggested to them that they had

failed to transmit to future generations any but fragments of their cherished past. . . . Diffuse and even irrational guilt plagued me until I had to laugh at myself. I had become a tasteless ethnic joke, paralyzed by Jewish guilt: about my relative youth and strength, about having a future where they did not, about my ability to come and go as I chose while they had to await my visits . . . , when I relished food that I knew that they could not digest, when I slept soundly through the night warmed by my husband's body, knowing the old people were sleeping alone in cold rooms. (In some African tribes, all the elderly are loaned a child for warmth and companionship at night.) (pp. 26-27)

This poignant mix of self-doubt and humor is reflected in many "tales of the field" (Van Maanen, 1988). When we become involved with our respondents, we invite them to be candid and even critical about our behavior—a one-way street in which we cannot reciprocate. Although feedback from respondents can be a valuable source of self-awareness, it can also be hurtful and frustrating (Daniels, 1983).

When we do need to vent frustrations, this is done off-site, preferably in a diary or with a peer support group where this information is "processed" as part of the study. The now-infamous diary of Bronislaw Malinowski (1967)—a founder of American ethnography—contained scathing references to the Trobriand Islanders with whom he lived as an ethnographer. Malinowski's petty but heartfelt complaints shocked many true believers and provided a valuable object lesson in the naïveté of assuming that the personal and professional could be kept separate during and after fieldwork.

The "shipboard romance" quality of the qualitative encounter (Daniels, 1983) has its advantages as well as disadvantages. Primarily, it fosters a type of candor and openness that qualitative researchers savor. Although often verging into close friendship by the end of the study, most qualitative research relationships are finite and goal directed. There is no question that the qualitative researcher is affected emotionally as well as intellectually by these relationships—the only real question is how these feelings are managed in the context of the study.

RESEARCHER-RESPONDENT DYNAMICS: GENDER, ETHNICITY, AGE, AND SOCIAL CLASS

The dynamic interplay between researchers and their respondents— each affecting one another in unforeseen ways—is one of the defining features of qualitative inquiry. Feminist researchers have led the way in discussing the impact of researcher subjectivity as a methodological issue (Fonow & Cook, 1991; Reinharz, 1992). Accepting rather than condemning its existence, they have explored how subjectivity shapes the study findings.

Although the researcher-respondent dyadic relationship can be influenced by many attributes, the most tangible are the "fit" (or lack thereof) in gender, ethnicity, age, and social class. Sometimes the researcher has little in common with his respondents. Elliot Liebow (1993) reflected on differences in sex, age, race, and social class when he began his study of African American homeless women in Washington, D.C. Yet he was able to forge enduring relationships with the homeless women and write a moving portrayal of their lives.

Rapport is hardly guaranteed by having a researcher-respondent match. Myerhoff was of the same sex and religion as her elderly Jewish respondents, but differences in age and lifestyle had to be overcome before she could be accepted by them. Feminist qualitative researchers have long noted that there are many occasions when shared gender is not enough to provide common ground (Hyde, 1994; Riessman, 1994).

A more pragmatic discussion of these factors and how they may be dealt with in entering the field will be offered in Chapter 5. Perhaps it is sufficient to say here that gender and other disparities in the researcher-researched dyad deserve close attention in qualitative research. A relationship of mutual respect need not be based on sameness. In most cases, the ultimate success of a qualitative study depends more on the skills of the researcher than on his demographic attributes.

SUMMARY AND CONCLUSION

The researcher-as-instrument is a defining characteristic of qualitative research. A qualitative researcher must be a do-it-yourselfer type, a person willing to take risks and rejection with good humor. Given the centrality of the researcher's role, personal qualities and skills come to the foreground as critical factors in the study's success or failure. You may not possess all of the traits and skills discussed in this chapter, but it is wise to reflect on your own capabilities before embarking on the journey.

Chapter 3

GETTING STARTED
Choosing a Topic and Designing the Study

For the social work researcher, there are so many potential topics of study that the choices seem endless. The setting can be in your own backyard or halfway around the world. The topic that you choose can arise from a number of places, including your own personal and professional interests. A particular area of social work practice may seem to cry out for qualitative inquiry. Or you may be driven by sheer intellectual curiosity about some aspect of the human condition totally unfamiliar to you.

There are two overarching considerations before you make your decision. First, your choice of qualitative methods should be driven by your research goals and objectives—not the other way around. One should not decide to do a qualitative study and then go search for a topic. Nor should the choice be driven by a mistaken assumption of expedience.

Second, clarify your epistemological stance early on. As we saw in Chapter 1, qualitative methods span a continuum of epistemological approaches ranging from accommodation with, to outright rejection of, logical positivism. It is important to locate where you are along this continuum and to be candid about this throughout the study. The best qualitative studies are situated within a known epistemological framework.

SELECTING A TOPIC: STUDYING
THE FAMILIAR VERSUS THE UNFAMILIAR

In its earliest years, qualitative research was synonymous with anthropological fieldwork in exotic locales—studies of the non-European

Other. Anthropologists were expected to go forth (for a year or more) and return with comprehensive accounts of life in different societies (most of which were undergoing rapid change as European colonies). Culture shock was part of the researcher's rite of passage. Studying one's own group or culture was a much lower priority, almost a waste of time.

Qualitative researchers have long since abandoned this premise—studies may take place at home or abroad. Thus, when contemplating doing a qualitative study, we face a critical juncture: do we choose to study the familiar or the unfamiliar (Ely et al., 1991)? Either choice entails risks and benefits, so the decision should be made carefully.

The temptation to study persons or situations that are familiar to us can be powerful. Many a valuable study has had its origins in personal biography: Irving Zola's (1983) struggle with physical disability, Catherine Riessman's (1990) exploration of divorcing couples, and Arlie Hochschild's (1989) study of working mothers are a few examples. Among students I have taught, studies of single fathers, interracial couples, and breast cancer survivors were motivated by personal concerns.

Professional interests and access may also play a role. Hence, teachers carry out studies in schools, nurses conduct research in hospitals, and academic psychologists study their undergrad students. For social workers, opportunities to study the familiar come from human service agencies where they are employed and from the clients they serve. This is all quite natural for clinically applied disciplines where the pursuit of knowledge meshes with the goal of improving practice.

There are two main advantages to studying the familiar:

1. *Easier entrée and development of rapport.* If you share your respondents' lifestyle or if you are already working in the agency or organization you seek to study, the path to acceptance and cooperation should be considerably smoother. The comfort levels of both you and your respondents are higher, making the beginning of the study much less intimidating for all concerned. This is no small benefit, as gaining access to a research site and to respondents can be very demanding for the qualitative researcher.

2. *A head start in knowledge about the topic.* If you are studying the familiar, you already have accumulated some knowledge about the subject, either through personal or professional experience.

Studying the familiar has its disadvantages, too. Perhaps the most obvious are the risks of being too close. For example, let us say that you are living with AIDS and have chosen to study support groups for persons with AIDS. In an interview with one of the group participants, he reveals that he refused to take protease inhibitors (or the latest promising drug therapy) when prescribed by his doctor. You are appalled, because you feel these drugs have saved your life. Can you keep the study on track without betraying your biases?

Or perhaps you are an agency administrator interested in an ethnographic study of your workplace and staff adaptations to new managed-care regulations. But the staff continue to see you as a boss and find it difficult to accept you in your new role. Relying on familiarity and personal assumptions are natural to the human condition, but they can blind us to new perspectives.

The remedy for this is straightforward: One must find a way to make the familiar unfamiliar (Ely et al., 1991). Observe the scene as an outsider, identify your assumptions as potential biases, and reassure your respondents that *you* are there to learn from *them*. The transition can be disconcerting, but it is essential.

Fascination with the unfamiliar can be a powerful and valuable motive for carrying out research. Studying the unfamiliar also offers several advantages. Assuming the vantage point of an outsider is certainly easier this way—the distance needed to discover implicit cultural rules and norms is built into the study. There is little or no role confusion—one enters and leaves the field as a researcher.

Of course, studying the unfamiliar can be risky. Just as we can know too much about the familiar, we may fall victim to ignorance (or even prejudices) about the unfamiliar. It is not difficult to see how stereotypes might interfere with studies of the Other—persons who do not share our gender, race, ethnicity, sexual orientation, or social class. Like most other professional groups, social workers (and social work researchers) are predominantly white and middle class in background. Our choice of client populations for study will naturally raise these concerns.

Gaining entrée and acceptance can be far more demanding when entering unfamiliar territory. One must negotiate with formal gatekeepers as well as individual respondents to enlist their cooperation and trust. For many researchers, the fear of rejection and humiliation by strangers can be paralyzing.

Reversing the process—making the unfamiliar familiar—requires patience and persistence (Ely et al., 1991). Avoiding stereotypical assumptions demands the same vigilance of self described earlier—monitoring one's own assumptions as potential sources of bias.

FORMULATING RESEARCH QUESTIONS

Regardless of where and with whom you decide to pursue qualitative research, be sure to choose a topic that excites you and that you can live with for months or even years. Once you have identified a topic and chosen qualitative methodology as the most appropriate mode of inquiry, the process of shaping a study begins. Unlike quantitative research with its goals of testing operational hypotheses using designs that unfold in a relatively orderly fashion, qualitative research questions and designs are messy, flexible, and not always predictable. They offer the greatest degree of discretionary authority for the researcher—providing maximal opportunity for creativity as well as the burden of decision making on an ongoing basis. Although qualitative researchers generally shun hypothesis testing, they may formulate working hypotheses or research questions to guide them in the study. These may or may not change over the course of the study.

DESIGNING THE STUDY

The phrase *research design* refers to the plans or procedures that allow the study's goals to be achieved. Both quantitative and qualitative research designs entail problem formulation, selecting a sample, collecting data, analyzing data, and writing up the findings. But the two approaches diverge in how flexibly these steps are carried out and in their prescribed sequencing.

The word *design* sounds almost too orderly for the sometimes messy process that unfolds in qualitative studies. Whereas quantitative researchers share a common language for designs (experimental, quasi-experimental, time-series, etc.), no such uniformity of classification exists among the diverse qualitative traditions (Tesch, 1990). Ignoring this Tower of Babel, most qualitative researchers simply describe in detail what they plan to do and how they plan to do it, using as many descriptors as apply (case study, ethnography, phenomenology, etc.).

Whereas some follow the orderly approach associated with grounded theory in sociology, others are inspired by interpretivist trends in the humanities to be more adventurous when designing the study (Janesick, 1994). As shown in Figure 3.1, qualitative research is distinguished by its *recursiveness* and *flexibility*. In contrast, quantitative research designs unfold in a more linear fashion; deviation from the design is considered a threat to the integrity and validity of the study.

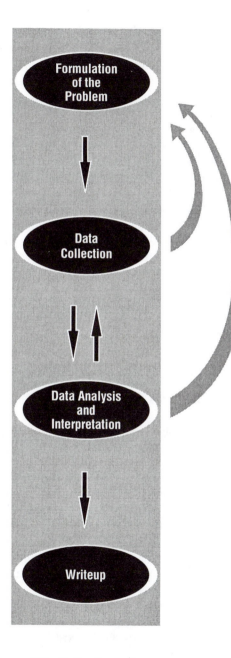

Figure 3.1. Phases of Qualitative Research

Qualitative researchers find themselves going back and forth between the stages of problem formulation, data collection, data analysis, and write-up. This process is rarely linear, but instead zigs and zags depending on where the data lead. In this fashion, the researcher may reformulate her research questions based on new findings, may seek new samples of respondents, and may pose new questions. Even the data analysis stage may precipitate a return to the field to collect new data.

This unique combination of flexibility and recursiveness makes many quantitative researchers uneasy. After all, in a quantitative study proposal, "what you see is what you get" (Morse, 1994). For better or worse, we are assured of a formulaic approach; control over bias is maximized by designs with high internal validity. With qualitative designs, "what you see is only loosely what you get." Where quantitative designs provide structure and guidance, qualitative researchers must convince their audience that they can produce credible, trustworthy findings. This, of course, focuses the spotlight on the researcher's abilities.

One way to enhance the credibility of a qualitative study is to carry out a *pilot study.* Even a small-scale pilot study can help smooth out wrinkles in the study's execution and enhance confidence in our ability to successfully complete the study.

WHEN ONE IS ENOUGH:
SINGLE CASE STUDIES

Single case studies have a long and honorable history in qualitative research (Feagin, Orum, & Sjoberg, 1991; Stake, 1994; Yin, 1994). Rather than portray a broad cross-section of individuals (or any other unit of analysis), case studies focus on "bounded systems of action" (Snow & Andersen, 1991, p. 152). Whether studies of an individual, an organization, or a whole city, single case studies draw on the maximal ability of the qualitative researcher to extract depth and meaning in context.

A psychiatric ward, a religious cult, a rural village, or a modern corporation can be the focus of a case study. Its goals may be thick description of the ethnographic present or of the historic past. The Lynds' sociological studies of *Middletown* (1937, 1956) are case studies of a community before and after the Great Depression that remain classics in the social science literature. Case studies also play an important role in program evaluation, where they are used to examine a program or agency as a bounded system of action (Greene, 1994).

Individuals who have led exemplary lives can provide a rich source of biographical material for exploring social and historical changes (Tuchman, 1994). Nell Irvin Painter's biography entitled *Hosea Hudson: His Life as a Negro Communist in the South* (1979) used interviews and archival materials to weave a portrait of the life of an African American radical in the early 20th century.

Regardless of its subject matter or goals, the case study draws on multiple perspectives and triangulated (or multiple) data sources (Snow & Andersen, 1991) to produce contextually rich information. Although a researcher might think that single case studies entail less data, a wealth of detail even from one person's life story can produce reams of data that require the same careful cataloguing and analysis as studies using multiple cases.

It is useful to distinguish *case studies in qualitative research* from *clinical case studies*. The latter are typically used to instruct and advance clinical practice—their primary purpose is pedagogic. In qualitative research, the case study method is not an educational or therapeutic tool, but a method of inquiry (Stake, 1994; Yin, 1994).

THE LITERATURE REVIEW: TO BE OR NOT TO BE?

Ideally, problem formulation takes place concurrently with reviewing the extant literature on the topic of interest. Some qualitative researchers eschew a literature review until after the findings are known, arguing that this distorts the emergent nature of the findings and puts unnecessary constraints on the free flow of ideas at the delicate, beginning stages of a study.

I believe that the advantages of consulting the literature and writing a review early on far outweigh the disadvantages. The literature review shapes the study, prevents reinventing the wheel, and promotes cumulative advances in knowledge. It situates the work in a scholarly context, ensuring that the study is linked to previous work in the area.

The conventions of literature reviews in qualitative research tend to favor informal language (including use of first-person pronouns) and freedom with literary styles of writing. However, a good review of the literature is a reasoned critical analysis regardless of whether it is situated in a quantitative or qualitative study. The researcher is obliged to examine ideas, develop themes, and show mastery. All worthwhile research begins with a convincing rationale for why it needs to be done, and a literature review is the best way to demonstrate this.

INTRODUCING TRIANGULATION

There are few concepts more central to understanding (and doing) qualitative research than the concept of *triangulation*. Although a more detailed discussion of triangulation will be offered in Chapter 8, it is useful to introduce the concept here to underscore its potential influence on qualitative studies in their formative stages.

The concept of triangulation in qualitative research refers to the convergence of multiple perspectives that can provide greater confidence that what is being targeted is being accurately captured. For example, when designing a study, you may want to consider pursuing multiple data sources. Diversifying sources of data and means of interpretation has value for enhancing the credibility of qualitative research findings.

A CONCLUDING NOTE
ON GETTING STARTED

This chapter has highlighted some of the many decisions a qualitative researcher must make before embarking on the journey. Answering the following basic questions gets the process going: (a) Are qualitative methods appropriate for my topic? (b) What is my epistemological stance in this study?

Once a topic has been identified, the researcher must choose between studying the familiar versus the unfamiliar, each approach carrying with it advantages and disadvantages. The next stages, formulating the research question(s), designing the study, writing the literature review, and carrying out a pilot study, require additional decision making, because qualitative methods are diverse and flexible.

In the following chapter, I will address a key issue in all research that poses special concerns for qualitative researchers—ethics and the protection of human subjects.

Chapter 4

ETHICAL ISSUES IN QUALITATIVE RESEARCH

Ethical issues arise in all types of research, and qualitative research is no exception. Indeed, the uniquely close, dynamic, and ongoing nature of the relationship between the researcher and respondent in qualitative research raises a number of ethical questions that quantitative researchers do not usually encounter (Punch, 1994).

Debates over research ethics have been especially lively among qualitative researchers who decry the objectification of human "subjects" in conventional scientific research. Some feminist researchers have even criticized qualitative methods such as in-depth interviewing as manipulative and exploitive (Oakley, 1981). Surely, there is no group more concerned about ethics and fairness in research than qualitative researchers.

The purpose of this chapter is to discuss the ethical implications of qualitative research, including issues more or less unique to this mode of inquiry and concerns that are common to many types of research designs. As we will see, institutional requirements for protecting human "subjects" are a necessary mechanism for ensuring that ethical qualitative research is carried out.

There is a type of moral ambiguity that accompanies naturalistic inquiry (Taylor, 1987). After all, we are studying people in their natural habitats, not in a pristine laboratory. Although ethical issues in qualitative research seldom if ever involve significant risks to human "subjects," research with vulnerable populations always requires vigilance—a delicate balancing act of learning while doing no harm.

The success of qualitative research depends on the ability of the researcher to become immersed in the world of the respondent and to be engaged in the field for a relatively long period of time. These essential qualities of *closeness* and *change over time* pose certain risks for the researcher as well as the researched. Although some ethical problems can be anticipated and dealt with in advance, the very flexibility of qualitative inquiry means that unforeseen dilemmas can arise at any time. Ethical problems can (and do) emerge from the uncontrolled, naturalistic settings where we conduct qualitative studies. Sometimes not taking action is more of an ethical problem than anything that we consciously do while engaged in the field (Taylor, 1987).

DECEPTION AND DISCLOSURE

The bulk of data in most qualitative studies is collected via observation and interviewing. Observation may run the gamut from full immersion (with an intense and ongoing relationship with the observed) to detached, unobtrusive studies of behavior in public places. A question that arises early on in a qualitative study using observation is whether some form of *deception* is necessary *and* is acceptable from an ethical standpoint. Deception can range from benign neglect (not telling persons in public places that they are being observed) to full deceit (concealing the nature of the study and the investigator's role) while interacting with respondents.

A number of valuable studies could not have been carried out without deception. LaPiere's (1934) study of racial and ethnic discrimination in the 1930s was based on his travels with a Chinese couple to various hotels and restaurants around the United States. The proprietors' discriminatory practices were, unbeknownst to them, contrasted with their previous survey responses stating they did not practice discrimination. If they had known the identity of LaPiere and his traveling companions, they probably would have behaved differently. Stanley Milgram's (1963) controversial psychological experiments demonstrating the distressingly common human capacity to inflict pain on others also depended on deception.

Researchers continue to disagree heartily about whether the risks of deception are worth the benefits. In this day and age, it is difficult to justify deception unless it is poses minimal or no risks. Whereas LaPiere's deception seems relatively benign, studies such as Milgram's—which used deception *and* caused emotional harm—are almost inconceivable today.

Some qualitative researchers strenuously object to any form of deception, but I see little harm in unobtrusive observation of nonsensitive public behavior when the identities of the observed are kept anonymous. If you are interested in how persons respond to panhandlers on the streets, asking the pedestrians and pandhandlers for their consent before they are observed would hardly make sense!

On the other hand, even studies in public places can be out of line if they involve sensitive behavior. Laud Humphries's (1970) research on gay men's behavior in public restrooms provoked cries of outrage when his deceptive tactics became known. Although Humphries countered that the study's findings justified the use of deception, few would defend his actions today. The lesson of Humphries's experience is simple: One should avoid covert studies of private or sensitive behaviors in public places, even if the participants' identities are kept anonymous.

As studies requiring deception are rare in social work, we have little need to agonize over this issue. Openness and full disclosure do not mean, however, that we must tell our respondents every detail of the study. Common sense dictates that we share the information necessary to inform potential respondents about the study and to gain rapport. Sharing too much information might prejudice respondents as well as burden them unnecessarily.

INFORMED CONSENT: CONDUCTING QUALITATIVE RESEARCH WITH VULNERABLE POPULATIONS

Because the vast majority of qualitative research involves active, face-to-face engagement, *informed consent* is a necessary prelude to beginning the relationship. The basic elements of informed consent are the following:

- A brief description of the study and its procedures as they involve participants (approximate number of interviews, duration of the study, etc.)
- Full identification of the researcher's identity and of the sponsoring organization (if any), including an address or telephone number for future contacts
- An assurance that participation is voluntary and the respondent has the right to withdraw at any time without penalty
- An assurance of confidentiality
- Any risks or benefits associated with participation in the study

It is convenient to have two copies of the consent form signed at the time consent is given (one for the researcher and one left with the respondent).

Special precautions are needed for studies involving members of vulnerable populations. For studies of children and adolescents under age 18, consent must be obtained from the parents *and* the child (children under age 12 may give verbal assent). For vulnerable adult populations such as the institutionalized elderly or seriously mentally ill, consent may need to be obtained from a guardian as well as the respondent.

Is signed consent always necessary? It may be waived under certain circumstances to protect the identities of vulnerable respondents. A researcher studying gay and lesbian youth at a gay-lesbian community center where they are considered emancipated would neither want nor need signed consent. The same would be true if you are studying undocumented immigrants who have reasonable fears that disclosing their identity would jeopardize their status.

In addition to obtaining consent from all respondents, the researcher must locate and get the permission of any *gatekeepers*. Gatekeepers are persons in authority whose approval is necessary to carry out the study. They can include agency directors, clinic supervisors, hospital administrators, school teachers, the local Board of Education, or the village chief. It is up to the researcher to know who the gatekeepers are and gain their cooperation (put into writing if possible). To neglect this important task could cause delays and even doom the study. It is also necessary to get explicit consent to use audiotapes or videotapes during the study.

Is informed consent necessary for off-the-cuff interviewing during observation in the field? During long periods of participant observation, it is only natural to ask questions of individuals while learning about the setting. These are usually spontaneous conversations initiated by the researcher. As such, they do not require formal consent, but they do imply *tacit consent* (because the respondent is free to refuse cooperation by simply walking away). For example, while observing a day-treatment center, you may have brief encounters with staff members to ask questions. Presumably, you have gotten permission from the center director (the gatekeeper) to carry out the study and staff have been informed of your purpose in being there. You will need to ask for written consent if the relationship becomes formalized, that is, if interviews are scheduled in advance and involve commitments of time and energy.

COERCION AND "DEFORMED" CONSENT

The threat of *coercion* is a genuine concern in social work research, especially when we study members of vulnerable populations. Our higher social position can inspire feelings of coercion (not to mention real coercion) that need to be addressed from the outset. (Otherwise, informed consent is really "deformed" consent.) For example, special care should be taken to assure respondents that they are free to refuse participation and to withdraw from the study at any time without any loss of services to which they are otherwise entitled.

For social work researchers, the potential for coercion becomes especially problematic when we seek to study our own clients, students, or work subordinates. For example, an administrator may want to conduct a study in her agency or a teacher may ask his students to participate in his research project. The latter example has been (and continues to be) the bread-and-butter of many an undergraduate psychology course.

Interrupting a professional relationship with one's client, student, or work subordinate to ask for consent can appear coercive even when handled sensitively. It can be hard on the prospective respondents (who do not want to displease us or who fear retribution) and it can be hard on us (trying to shift between research and work roles). Ideally, we should obtain consent *before* the professional relationship begins.

As I argued in Chapter 1, qualitative research is incompatible with the practice mandate when the practitioner is also the researcher. I can see no satisfactory way to blend the two roles, because the demands of being a practitioner preclude the free flow of information and openness of inquiry that are the essence of qualitative research. Teachers and agency supervisors are similarly constrained when they consider studying their students or subordinates.

There are no easy answers here, but I believe a reasonable position can be stated as follows: Although it is not inherently unethical to do so, qualitative researchers should avoid studying their clients, students, and work subordinates. By doing so, we not only avoid the risk of coercion, but we maximize the benefits of qualitative inquiry *and* of clinical practice.

DISTRESS AND EMOTIONAL HARM

Obtaining uncoerced informed consent does not prevent another ethical problem from arising during qualitative research—emotional distress. Many qualitative interviews elicit intense discussions of painful life events such as divorce, death of a family member, and domestic abuse. Sensitivity to research ethics dictates that we do not introduce these topics gratuitously; they should either be volunteered by the respondents or inquired about when they are the focus of the study. Extremely sensitive topics (incest, child abuse, suicidality, homicidality) must be handled with extreme care. In some cases, they may even require the researcher to take action by notifying the appropriate authorities.

Much depends on the skill and sensitivity of the interviewer. If the researcher plans to inquire about emotion-laden topics, she should make arrangements for referrals to professional counseling when necessary. If a trained clinician, she should not provide this assistance herself (even if respondents directly request it). Thus, if a parent asks for advice about how to deal with a schizophrenic child or a couple seeks your counsel about marital problems, help them find the necessary services and leave the service provision to others.

Displays of emotional distress by respondents are not uncommon, but they are usually transient and rarely disrupt the interview relationship. Rather than resent the qualitative researcher for eliciting such feelings, most respondents remark that the interview is an emotional catharsis for them, a chance to express themselves to a nonjudgmental, sympathetic listener.

On those rare occasions when a respondent needs help for emotional problems, the researcher can provide a list of agencies or referral sources at the close of the interview. The same can be done when respondents ask for assistance with medical or social services problems. For example, in the New York University-Georgetown University Mammogram Study in which I am involved (heretofore known as the Mammogram Study), one of the respondents asked the interviewer for help in finding out if she was eligible for Medicaid. Soon after, the interviewer contacted her with the information. Although no respondents have asked for assistance in obtaining mental health treatment, we are prepared to offer referral information if they do.

CONFIDENTIALITY AND PRIVACY

Unlike quantitative researchers who provide "safety in numbers" for their respondents, qualitative researchers cannot guarantee *anonymity* because the respondent is known (and known well) by the researcher. By agreeing to participate in the study, respondents sacrifice anonymity and usually a good deal of privacy as well.

For nonclinical researchers, the guarantee of *confidentiality* should remain absolute. Every effort should be made to ensure that the identities of our respondents are never revealed. They should rest assured that the researcher will never link them to the information they provide during the study without their permission. Breaches of confidentiality—one of the utmost violations of trust—must be due only to dire circumstances where there are serious risks of harm to others.

For clinical researchers, there is one clear exception to the rule of confidentiality—the legal requirement of mandated reporting. Licensed clinicians carrying out research must follow the laws regarding mandated reporting of child abuse and should state this on the consent form. Although this warning may deter some participants from giving consent to be in the study, it is a necessary precaution.

What if a respondent reports contemplating homicide or suicide or some other violent act? If such behavior seems probable and imminent, the researcher may wish to breach the promise of confidentiality and go to the proper authorities. The research relationship is not worth ignoring evidence of dangerousness to self or to others.

Sometimes our respondents are involved in activities that are not dangerous but are still illegal, for example, shoplifting, prostitution, drug use, or truancy from school. Qualitative researchers cannot allow their personal or moral concerns about these behaviors to interfere with the promise of confidentiality. Interceding to prevent such activities would not likely be successful and in any case would end the research relationship (and possibly any chance of learning more about these behaviors).

The nature of qualitative reports makes guaranteeing confidentiality harder than it seems. The dilemma arises when our efforts to disguise our respondents' identities are not effective enough. Confidentiality during data collection requires using code numbers or pseudonyms rather than names on all notes and tapes. For the write-up, we use pseudonyms and may change inconsequential facts in the vignettes to prevent the reader from discerning who we are talking about. We may do this when referring to the research site as well.

INCENTIVES AND PAYBACK

Small monetary payments or gifts encourage participation and compensate respondents for their time. Most funded research projects include such payments in their budgets. In our Mammogram Study, we paid respondents 25 dollars after the interview was completed.

The decision about how much to pay respondents is an ethical one. If we pay too little, the incentive value is lost and we risk insulting them. But if we pay too much (and especially if our prospective respondents are poor), we risk coercion by "purchasing" their cooperation. Novice researchers usually consult with their more experienced colleagues to learn about the current rates of compensation paid to respondents. The size of the incentive payment usually depends on how much is being asked of the respondent in terms of time and inconvenience.

Of course, payment of incentives is not feasible for many qualitative researchers who do not have funding, especially students who are themselves struggling financially. In these instances, we compensate for the absence of incentives by relying on the kindness of strangers—a kindness that is usually extended to the well-meaning researcher.

Another form of compensation can come during the study, a natural consequence of prolonged engagement. For example, a colleague of mine conducting an ethnographic study of a case-management program for persons with serious mental illness offered much-needed computer assistance to project staff (L. Francis, personal communication, 1995). Similarly, we can make ourselves useful by being a "gofer," carrying out menial but useful tasks for our respondents as they go about their lives and labors. This reflects the naturally subordinate position of the qualitative researcher in the field—a humbling experience for those of us accustomed to a modicum of professional deference.

Payback during the study also includes the provision of information and referrals for social or therapeutic services at the close of the interview. At the least, it involves a sympathetic ear during quasi-therapeutic encounters.

An overlooked and seldom-discussed source of payback occurs after the study is completed—the ethical requirement to write up the findings and share them with respondents and other intended audiences (Wolcott, 1994). Researchers who ask for the time and good will of strangers fail in the ethics department when they willfully ignore this requirement. Respondents often want (and always deserve) to see the products of our labors.

RISKS TO THE RESEARCHER: DEALING WITH EMOTIONS AND MORAL AMBIGUITY

Although the paramount concern in all research lies with protecting respondents from harm, there are emotional and other risks for the researcher that need mention. By anticipating and dealing with these risks, we are in a better position to protect our respondents as well as ourselves.

The most immediate concern for the researcher is emotional. Because we are engaged in the same emotionally intense encounters as our respondents, it would be impossible to avoid experiencing ups and downs during fieldwork. Furthermore, we experience many such encounters over a period of time with different respondents, so the cumulative impact of intensive field research can be exhausting.

What if a respondent's comments strike an emotional nerve—touching on the researcher's own fears of abandonment, illness, or death? You may find yourself interviewing an older woman dying of cancer and thinking of your own mother's death last year. What if a young woman's story of childhood sexual abuse stirs painful memories of your own childhood trauma? It is difficult to escape self-reflection and a flood of emotions when a respondent's story hits home.

In these instances, it is wise to practice *bracketing* (Ely et al., 1991). Bracketing refers to a conscientious (and constant) effort to suspend our assumptions, beliefs, and feelings in order to better understand the experience of our respondents. In qualitative research, we do not seek to eliminate or repress our beliefs and feelings, but to identify them so that they do not interfere with the study.

Emotional stress is not the only risk a qualitative researcher may encounter. Although extremely rare, threats to physical safety may come from respondents, especially those with violent histories. Sexual come-ons and innuendo are not uncommon either. These can be most discomfiting, as interviews often take place in the respondent's home or in some other private location where the researcher can feel vulnerable.

Feelings of closeness and intimacy may lead respondents to go over the line. In her study of divorcing couples, Riessman (1990) found herself on several occasions deflecting sexual advances by male respondents. Similarly, Weiss (1994) reported that female respondents made sexual overtures to him on several occasions. Needless to say, dealing with these threats requires professional poise and firmness. If a respondent's behavior becomes in any way physically or sexually threatening, the researcher should not hesitate to exit the scene as safely and as quickly as possible.

There are also times when respondents tell us things that appall or anger us. It is not uncommon to have to endure a stream of sexist, racist, and homophobic invective in the course of an interview. Respondents may boast of exploits that strike us as potentially harmful or self-destructive. Sometimes they make decisions that cause bafflement and dismay. A student of mine studying mothers with AIDS was shocked to hear some of the women say that they did not intend to tell their children about their illness. She could not understand how a mother could withhold such vital information from her own child and had to restrain herself mightily to keep from showing her true feelings.

The decision to intervene is rarely easy and frequently has unforeseen consequences. Steven J. Taylor (1987) described in detail a difficult situation he encountered: physical and verbal abuse of mentally retarded adults by the attendants in a residential facility where he was conducting fieldwork. Although appalling, the attendants' behavior triggered a moral dilemma for Taylor when he reviewed his options for responding.

Intervening with the attendants might have inhibited their abusive behavior (at least in Taylor's presence), but at a cost of breaching confidentiality and losing rapport (thereby ending his inhibiting presence *and* the study). Blowing the whistle and notifying the authorities (facility administrators, the police, or the media) was made complicated by the fact that facility administrators knew about the abuse, tolerated it, and even covered it up when confronted by family members. Taylor noted that pointing the finger at a few attendants was not likely to prevent future abuse because it was so prevalent and tolerated. Blowing the whistle also comes at a cost—breaching confidentiality and effectively ending the study.

Although acknowledging that there are occasions when intervening is worth it, Taylor ultimately decided to take no immediate action against any specific individuals (thereby protecting confidentiality). Instead, he carefully documented his observations. After completing the study and writing about the prevalence of institutionalized abuse in treatment of the mentally retarded (Taylor & Bogdan, 1980), he led a media campaign to expose the abuse and worked with legal advocacy groups to draw attention to its prevalence. What at first seemed morally unacceptable—continuing the study—gave him the commitment and knowledge to pursue these activities (Taylor, 1987).

The ethical issue for qualitative researchers in these situations is not *whether* to do something, but *what, how* and *when* to do it. The lesson of Taylor's experience is that initial impulses to dive in and do something should be weighed against all foreseeable consequences.

Researchers working in noninstitutional settings may experience moral ambiguity as well. What if a woman with an abnormal Pap smear tells you that she will not seek further treatment because she fears it will make her infertile? Or a gang member describes an upcoming initiation rite involving gang rape? Or an immigrant mother tells you that she is looking for a doctor to perform female circumcision on her infant daughter? The options here are the same as Taylor's: do nothing, end the study relationship, intervene with the respondent, or blow the whistle to the authorities. There are times when we must control our impulse to intervene and other times when the need to protect others from harm requires immediate action. Unfortunately, there are no clear-cut rules for which course of action to take and when to take it.

THE BIGGER PICTURE: SOCIALLY RESPONSIBLE RESEARCH AS ETHICAL RESEARCH

Most discussions of ethics in research focus on protecting individual participants from harm. Even when we suspend or defer the helping mandate during research, we always seek to preserve our respondents' dignity and humanity. But social work researchers are also attuned to the bigger picture and to the need for social responsibility in research. In the broadest sense, socially responsible research is congruent with social work values of respect for human rights and concern for social justice.

Despite its tendency to focus on people's lives in microscopic detail, qualitative research (like all research) takes place within a larger socio-political context that is laden with meaning. Social responsibility includes being sensitive to diversity—gender, social class, age, ethnicity, and sexual orientation. Here, qualitative research has a distinct advantage. Like their practitioner colleagues, qualitative researchers "go where the respondents are." The complex textures of gender, ethnic, and other identities are not subverted but celebrated. (Of course, even qualitative researchers can wittingly or unwittingly allow bias against diversity to creep into the study.)

Attention to social responsibility in qualitative research is particularly relevant at the beginning and end of the research process. By selecting a topic for study that has the potential to improve people's lives and by writing up and disseminating the findings to a larger audience, we are fulfilling our ethical obligations as researchers who care about human concerns.

If we are worried that our findings will be misused by conservative powers-that-be, we can help to frame the presentation of the results and discuss their implications. A study finding that parents have problems coping with children suffering from schizophrenia need not support those calling for psychiatric reinstitutionalization. Instead, we can point to the parents' resilience and to the success of psychoeducational support groups (McFarlane, Link, Dushay, Marchal, & Crilly, 1994) and other support mechanisms that ease the burden of care.

Socially responsible research does not mean presenting a one-sided portrait that leaves out the less savory aspects of respondents' lives. Whereas we are not investigative reporters digging for dirt, neither are we seeking an uplifting portrayal devoid of reality. This delicate balance between accuracy and sensitivity to respondents' needs affects studies of the despicable, the heroic, and the everyday people in between.

SUMMARY AND CONCLUSION

Ethical issues are woven throughout qualitative research (Ely et al., 1991). Furthermore, our studies are conducted in a sociopolitical context that should not be ignored. Our integrity as researchers depends on honoring our ethical responsibilities at both the microlevel (protecting our respondents) and the macrolevel (selecting socially responsible topics, disseminating the findings, and protecting them from misuse whenever possible).

The vast majority of ethical problems we face in qualitative studies are no more severe than those we encounter in everyday life (Lofland & Lofland, 1995). Indeed, qualitative researchers can take comfort in the fact that our studies rarely pose risk. More often, they provide a genuinely satisfying experience for respondents. In any case, our abiding wish is to do no harm (Weiss, 1994).

Chapter 5

ENTERING THE FIELD AND SAMPLING STRATEGIES

To paraphrase anthropologist Rosalie Wax (1971), anyone unprepared to make mistakes, be embarrassed, and feel like a fool should think twice before embarking on the qualitative journey of discovery. Even for experienced qualitative researchers, entering the field takes fortitude. Here and elsewhere, I use the term "field" to refer to the process of actively carrying out qualitative research, more a state of mind than a particular locale.

In early ethnographies, the field typically referred to a faraway village where anthropologists went to spend long periods of time learning about the local culture. In social work qualitative research, the field may refer to a setting such as a hospital emergency room, to a series of interviews held at various locales, to a library or archives, or to all of these. What distinguishes being in or out of the field is the stage of the research vis-à-vis data collection.

Given the wide variety in places where social work researchers go to do research, it is a challenge to offer general guidelines for entering the field. Nevertheless, there are some commonalities. In every case, the researcher wishes to gain entry, develop rapport, and proceed to sampling and data collection with a minimum of problems. In this chapter I will address these activities in turn, reserving the next chapter (Chapter 6) for more in-depth discussion of data collection.

TACTICS FOR GAINING ENTRY: DEPENDING ON THE KINDNESS OF STRANGERS

After spending time developing ideas and a proposal to carry out a qualitative study, the researcher may be hesitant to take the plunge and venture out into the unknown world of data collection. Now the cerebral gives way to the social. At times, it may seem easier to return to your desk and contemplate the written word in solitude. Steeling oneself for a foray that could result in rejection or humiliation is not easy. On the other hand, one can only learn qualitative research by doing it. A mixture of tact, persistence, patience, flexibility, and humor are the necessary ingredients for success.

If you have chosen to study the familiar, gaining entrée is likely to be easier. Personal acquaintance with key respondents or with the site of the study can smooth the way considerably. However, it is best not to take anything for granted. A friendly administrator or agency you have worked with in the past may bristle at the prospect of being put under scrutiny in the name of research.

If you have chosen to study the unfamiliar, you will want to plan a strategy that maximizes your acceptance. Remember that it is incumbent on the researcher to demonstrate that the study is valuable and feasible. Many respondents have little to gain and fear they have much to lose by cooperating with researchers. Although students conducting research are often granted more latitude and acceptance than professors, no researcher can assume cooperation to be forthcoming. Ultimately, you are depending on the kindness of strangers.

If your desired respondents are part of a hierarchical organization, finding the gatekeeper(s) and getting permisson is an essential first step. The gatekeeper could be an agency administrator, a physician, a program director, a school principal, a teacher, a parent, or any other authority figure who controls access to a site or to respondents. Beyond giving necessary permission, the enthusiastic endorsement of a gatekeeper can be enormously helpful.

In approaching gatekeepers, the researcher should be direct and forthright about the study's goals and its potential benefits (as well as risks). It is especially important to inform gatekeepers and respondents about the time-consuming nature of qualitative research. With few exceptions, one may safely assume that their knowledge of being a research participant is nonexistent.

Formal permission at the outset of the study is only the beginning. Gaining entry and maintaining rapport are ongoing processes that do not end until the study is over. Unlike quantitative surveys where one-shot data collection brings a minimum of contact, qualitative research demands immersion and engagement. Research relationships may have to be negotiated and renegotiated as needed.

ASSUMING A STANCE: PRESENTATION
OF SELF IN THE FIELD

Even before entering the field, it is advisable to clarify what stance you will take vis-à-vis your respondents. Qualitative researchers vary greatly in how they present themselves (Schatzman & Strauss, 1973). Erving Goffman (1959), for example, adopted a marginal stance, detaching himself as he observed asylums and other institutions. His role as a researcher, although relatively unobtrusive, was unmistakable. At the other end of the continuum, many feminist researchers advocate a research partnership in which roles are blurred and researchers are actively engaged with respondents (Reinharz, 1992).

The researcher is obliged to enter the field "with an open mind, not an empty head" (Fetterman, 1989, p. 11). Although the respondent is considered the expert, the researcher should be knowledgeable about the topic at hand. In her study of women with breast cancer, Anne S. Kasper (1994) noted that interrupting an interview to ask "what is breast reconstructive surgery?" would be an unacceptable breach of protocol. Similarly, Manwar, Johnson, and Dunlap (1994) learned the lingo of the drug world before beginning their study of New York City crack dealers.

With knowledgeability also comes engagement, especially when *in vivo* observation is used. Of course, the degree of participation depends on the context. Eliot Liebow (1993) spent many hours at a homeless women's shelter where he shared in the daily activities of women residents. He did not become homeless himself, but he was far from a detached observer. Similarly, Sue Estroff (1981) carried out ethnographic research among persons with schizophrenia by sharing in virtually all aspects of their daily lives. She even took Prolixin to experience firsthand the drug's side effects (a degree of immersion few of us would be willing to undertake).

There will always be qualitative studies where full (or even partial) participation is undesirable—studies of heroin addicts, car thieves, and sexual abusers come readily to mind. Although rapport can be gained by assuming a nonjudgmental stance, the researcher's role as an outsider is crystal clear.

Given the dynamic nature of qualitative research, our position on the continuum of participation versus detachment may fluctuate over the course of a study. Some settings and some respondents may elicit more interaction and sharing than others. It is not easy to predict how the "fit" between researcher and respondent will play out.

Issues of Gender, Race, and Social Class

The researcher's gender, race, and social class are statuses that present potential advantages as well as disadvantages for the qualitative researcher seeking acceptance in the field. As discussed in Chapter 2, the qualitative researcher assumes a reflexive stance, anticipating as much as possible how his or her personal qualities may impinge upon the study.

Mutable characteristics of the researcher, such as dress, demeanor, and interviewing style are important, but can be adjusted to fit the situation. It is our ascribed traits—gender, race, and age—that require serious consideration because they are immutable and laden with meaning. Socially constructed meanings associated with gender, race, and age—no matter how arbitrary—come into sharp relief in qualitative research, where relationships are marked by closeness and long duration.

In her study of psychiatric outpatients living in the community, Sue Estroff (1981) offered these observations:

> Being female helped and hurt. Over half of the subjects were men. My gender served as an entree to contacting them and eliciting some interest, but it created tensions as well. Many had never had a female friend, that is, a symmetrical, platonic, heterosexual relationship. This led to some confusion on their part when their sexual advances offended me, and to reluctance on my part in entering situations . . . which might be misconstrued. (p. xvii)

Some researchers advocate *matching* interviewers with respondents. Defenders of matching tend to cite greater *acceptability* and *understandability* as two primary advantages (Weiss, 1994). In our Mammogram Study, where topics ranged from body image to racism, it was considered essential to recruit African American women as interviewers, and we believe that rapport and richness of data were enhanced considerably by this decision. However, matching has its pros and cons. This issue will be addressed in greater detail in Chapter 6 on data collection.

Researcher Disclosure: How Much Is Enough? Too Much?

When entering the field, how much should the researcher reveal about the study? About him or herself? Qualitative researchers generally adhere to advice to be "truthful but vague" (Taylor & Bogdan, 1984). Of course, one should not lie if directly asked a question about the study. But there is considerable discretion in deciding how much to reveal.

Disclosure also encompasses details about the researcher's background and personal life. Here again, there is a continuum: whereas some researchers suggest providing the basic "business card" information (Weiss, 1994), others argue that sharing personal information encourages fuller disclosure by respondents and promotes an egalitarian partnership between the researcher and respondent (Reinharz, 1992).

Personal disclosure is especially easy when we are studying the familiar. Catherine Riessman (1990) reported that sharing her divorced single-parent status with her respondents enhanced their willingness to talk about their own experiences with divorce. When one is studying the unfamiliar, some personal information may humanize the researcher and make her less intimidating as an outsider. This is particularly helpful in studies of client populations—persons whose backgrounds usually differ from our own.

Some degree of personal disclosure is almost unavoidable in qualitative research. How much you self-disclose depends on your respondents' wishes and sensitivities and your own comfort level. However, keep in mind that the study is not about you, but about your respondents and their lives.

SAMPLING STRATEGIES IN QUALITATIVE RESEARCH

Because one cannot study everything and everyone, sampling strategies with clear rationales are needed. As with quantitative research, sampling decisions are critical. However, sampling in qualitative research is directed to differing ends and proceeds from different assumptions. Here, the focus is on flexibility and depth rather than on mathematical probabilities and generalizability. The phrase that quantitative research is "a mile wide and an inch deep," and qualitative research is "an inch wide and a mile deep" holds a grain of truth when it comes to sampling.

Compared with quantitative sampling strategies, qualitative sampling involves much smaller numbers (even $N = 1$) and nonprobability techniques (e.g., purposive, convenience, and snowball sampling).Whereas quantitative sampling seeks to recreate the total population "in miniature" (Weiss, 1994), qualitative studies sample to capture depth and richness rather than representativeness.

Sampling in qualitative studies is also an interactive process where respondents may be sought based on questions arising from the data analyses. For example, many qualitative researchers immersed in data analysis purposefully return to the field to select "negative" or "disconfirming" cases to test their emergent hypotheses (Morse, 1994).

Qualitative researchers feel no need to apologize for sampling strategies that make quantitative researchers cringe. Whereas the latter focus on the bulge in the bell curve, searching for normative patterns, qualitative researchers often choose to focus on the "outliers," the atypical cases that remind us of the richness of human diversity. Of course, we must deal with the implications of these sampling strategies because we live in a quantitative world. It should come as no surprise that qualitative studies tend to have a built-in bias toward respondents who are sociable *and* verbal. Qualitative researchers are also subject to accusations of "stacking the deck," that is, selecting respondents to fit their preconceived notions.

I find that one of the more difficult aspects of doing qualitative research is explaining to skeptical colleagues that qualitative sampling should not be judged by quantitative standards.This is not to say that qualitative researchers are unconcerned about bias. We do not argue that our samples are broadly representative or that our findings are generalizable to other groups or sites. Instead, we seek *corroboration* for our findings from other sources (more on this in Chapter 8).

SELECTING THE SITE

The choice of a site for a qualitative study usually represents a balance of research interests and availability. Whether you veer toward the familiar or the unfamiliar, this choice should be carefully made. As noted by

Marshall and Rossman (1995), some studies are site-specific and imply interest in an organizational setting or program, for example, a mental health clinic, a battered women's shelter, or a school for deaf children. In these instances, the selection of a site logically proceeds from the study's aims.

Studies that are targeted to populations (e.g., teenage mothers, substance abusers, or the chronically ill elderly) or phenomena (e.g., child abuse, religious fundamentalism, or managed care) may require greater mobility as the researcher must operate at multiple sites.

Although access and availability are key criteria in site selection, the researcher should not let convenience alone dictate where the study takes place. In short, the site should fit the study, not the other way around. The temptation to conduct qualitative research in one's backyard should not override the need to get rich and valuable information.

SELECTING STUDY RESPONDENTS

Qualitative researchers can (and do) sample any number of things: sites (such as agencies) and events (such as meetings or psychotherapy sessions) as well as people. In this section, I will focus on the latter.

In general, qualitative researchers pursue some form of *purposive* or *theoretical* sampling—selecting respondents based on their ability to provide needed information. If, for example, you are interested in how a cancer patient copes with pain, you will do better to seek out respondents who have pain than to attempt a random sampling of an oncologist's patient roster. Or, if you are interested in a client's subjective experience of psychotherapy, you are likely to select persons who are articulate and introspective enough to provide you with a description of their experience.

Like their quantitative counterparts, qualitative researchers also use *convenience* sampling, that is, selecting respondents based on their availability. Although this should exclude using one's own friends and relatives, exploiting personal or professional networks to recruit respondents is a common strategy, especially when the target group is difficult to track down. For example, a single father interested in studying other single fathers might ask for referrals from members of his support group. In this way, a sample is gradually accrued by *snowball sampling.*

Oftentimes, qualitative researchers must "go where the respondents are" to recruit them into the study. These locations could be gay bars, support-group meetings, beauty shops, churches, homeless shelters, or any site where would-be respondents congregate. Gaining the cooperation of gatekeepers can be critical in some instances.

Finally, qualitative researchers may *advertise* for volunteers. (Human subjects protection committees are especially fond of this approach, as it eliminates coercion.) Advertising is particularly useful in locating members of vulnerable populations who are unreachable by conventional means of recruitment. Often, gatekeepers are reluctant or even forbidden to assist researchers in making direct contacts with these individuals. Let us say, for example, that you are interested in studying infertile couples, and the fertility specialist you contact is unwilling to assist in directly recruiting couples for your study. An alternative route is to post a notice in the specialist's office waiting area describing the study and soliciting volunteers.

In practice, qualitative researchers may resort to any or all of these means of recruiting respondents into a study. Creativity and ingenuity are needed, along with the requisite sensitivity to ethical concerns discussed in Chapter 4.

HOW MANY DO I NEED?

When asked this question by students in quantitative research classes, I respond by talking about numbers of variables and statistical power analyses (mixed with a bit of common sense regarding time and resources available for the study). In my qualitative methods course, I try to forestall even being asked this question. The reason is probably apparent by now: There is no way of knowing for sure. However, to produce a credible proposal, the qualitative researcher should provide an approximate estimate of sample size (and then go on to explain the flexible nature of qualitative research sampling techniques).

Perhaps it is sufficient to say that sample sizes in qualitative studies can range from one to as many as the researcher needs (and can pursue given the constraints of time and resources). For certain types of qualitative approaches such as case studies and life history, only one or a few respondents may be enough. For most other types of studies, the number of respondents is considerably larger (Morse, 1994). Because the emphasis is on quality rather than quantity, qualitative researchers sample not to maximize numbers, but to become "saturated" with information about a specific topic.

RECRUITING AND RETAINING RESPONDENTS

Like their quantitative counterparts, qualitative researchers recruit respondents by identifying themselves and by explaining the purpose of the study in general terms, including its potential benefits and risks. A good deal of charm and gentle persuasion goes a long way to facilitate this process. When available, gatekeeper permission can be invoked to lend the study further credibility.

Key informants (knowledgeable insiders) can help us informally throughout the study, particularly when we are studying the unfamiliar. Anthropologists have always depended heavily on them to assist in understanding local norms and to help in identifying promising respondents. Many researchers remain friends with their key informants long after leaving the field, forever indebted to them for their help.

Recruiting and retaining respondents is enhanced considerably by the use of incentives such as small amounts of money or gifts. If the study is funded by a grant, this is automatically included in the budget and involves no personal expense. When the investigator is impoverished or underfunded, incentives can be replaced by in-kind contributions.

The qualitative researcher should provide a compelling case for the study, play the humble role of an eager learner, and respond professionally and maturely to suspicion and outright rejection. In addition to good interpersonal skills, the researcher is well advised to exercise political and social savvy—be alert to the sociocultural and political context of the study. Many organizations and individuals are understandably skeptical about research and its benefits. Even when formal permission is granted by a gatekeeper, resistance and sabotage by uncooperative staff or family members may await the unwary researcher.

Researchers must also be mindful of the potentially damaging effects of their presence on respondents' lives. In her study of female police officers, Teri Friedman (1991) learned that her respondents were subjected to ostracism by their fellow officers—a painful but unforeseen consequence that can occur when we study any close-knit, suspicious group.

I do not wish to convey an alarmist viewpoint here. In my experience, even the most skeptical research participants usually warm quickly to the attentions of a qualitative researcher. Even agencies in the midst of crises often welcome having a "third party" around to witness their efforts and provide moral support. But it is incumbent upon the researcher to keenly observe the context of the study, to be sensitive to local norms, and to know when to pull back.

SUMMARY AND CONCLUSION

Entering the field—plunging into the real world of empirical data collection—clearly has its hazards and challenges. Taking that first step in approaching a site or a respondent may be an extrovert's dream, but for most of us it takes steely fortitude. Even when we choose to study the familiar, we must present our "research" selves and ask our respondents to accept this change with equanimity.

Despite all of its pitfalls and potential humiliations, entering the field brings to life what qualitative research is all about—venturing forth to learn and grow.

Chapter 6

DATA COLLECTION

There are three basic modes of data collection in qualitative research: (a) *observation* (of the respondent, the setting, and oneself), (b) *interviewing*, and (c) *review of documents or archival materials*. Although each of these will be discussed in turn, they are interrelated and often occur simultaneously.

Students unfamiliar with qualitative methods often assume that intensive interviewing is the sole mode of data collection. However, qualitative research entails more than interviewing. As noted by Spradley (1979) and Ely et al. (1991), interviewing cannot be divorced from observing, interacting, and noting what is happening while the researcher is in the field. Archival materials, when available and relevant to the study's goals, are another source of information. For some studies, interviews are primary and observation is secondary and for other studies the opposite is true.

OBSERVATION

Although observation in the field is responsible for the popular mystique of qualitative methods (dating back to the heyday of anthropological studies by Margaret Mead and others), it is the least familiar mode of qualitative data collection. Social work practitioners are trained to be keen observers of their clients, but their observational goals are quite different from those of qualitative research.

Despite volumes of "field wisdom" passed on by generations of ethnographers (Sanjek, 1990), the demands of qualitative observation can only be appreciated by hands-on experience. Students in my qualitative methods course react quite similarly during their first participant-observation assignment. When asked to spend one hour in an unfamiliar public place and record all that they see, the initial response is "how easy" and "what a nice break from our usual class assignments." Then they go out to do it. Returning to the classroom with their fieldnotes, they express surprise (stopping just short of amazement) that such an "easy assignment" could be so demanding. Comments run along these lines: "I couldn't decide what to write down," "there was so much going on, I didn't know where to start," "I've never had to do anything like this before."

We all have a bit of the participant observer in us. Our observations are especially keen when we enter new situations where it is natural to examine the surroundings and locate the key players. But qualitative research demands a more systematic, thorough, and nonjudgmental form of observation that few neophyte researchers have experienced.

Whether one chooses *participant observation* or a more detached observational stance depends in large part on one's study goals. Participant observation lies at the more intensive end of the continuum of involvement, a technique long honored in anthropology. It is always a memorable, and oftentimes humbling, experience. Anthropologists enjoy sharing harrowing tales of finding themselves in a muddy Amazonian village or a frozen Aleut encampment with a few notebooks and a year's supply of peanut butter. Of course, one need not travel to a far-away exotic locale to be a participant observer. Closer to home, ethnographers of surgeons (Bosk, 1979), psychiatric clients (Estroff, 1981), and homeless women (Liebow, 1993) have their own stories of seeking entry into a new social world (with perhaps a few more of the comforts of home).

Some qualitative researchers keep participation to a minimum, either by preference or as dictated by the setting. Unobtrusive observation in public places corresponds to the latter approach. When concerned about *reactivity*, qualitative researchers tend to minimize their own involvement whenever possible.

The decision to pursue or avoid participation, like other aspects of qualitative research, may be modified as the study goes on. The desire to capture "natural" behavior may lead you to prefer a detached stance at the outset of the study. Moreover, entering the field as an enthusiastic participant may only highlight your position as an outsider and alienate your informants. Common sense dictates that the researcher's stance should be congruent with the surroundings and shifted along the continuum of involvement as necessary.

Recording Observational Data

Just as the researcher's eyes and ears capture the salient information, her fieldnotes contain a record of what has been observed. But what does one look for? The best approach, advocated by experts in ethnographic techniques (Agar, 1980; Marshall & Rossman, 1995; Spradley, 1979; Wolcott, 1988) is to begin by casting a wide net and then move to more focused observation as the study's analytic themes crystallize.

What is important to avoid is a reliance on preexisting ideas, theories, or categories (and to acknowledge this when it occurs). This can happen in "first-order" field observations of persons, for example, referring to a man and a woman arguing in a park as a "couple" without knowing their relationship status. It can also occur when we are prejudging the behavior of others, for example, interpreting an interviewee's reluctance to address a sensitive issue as "denial" or "repression."

Taking *fieldnotes,* an essential task of the observer in the field, provides us with data for later analysis (Agar, 1980). Much has been written addressing the "why, what, and how" questions of field note-taking. Answering "why" is easy: logging one's observations produces valuable raw data that can lead to more focused follow-up via interviewing or additional observation.

The "what" of field note-taking depends on your topic of interest as no one person can record everything. "Thick" description—logging as much as possible without an interpretative filter—is the goal. General suggestions for what to look for in the initial phase of field observation include physical space, actors, behaviors, interactions, relationships, and expressions of feelings or emotions. If one is observing a bounded physical space, it is useful to draw a map of the space to form the backdrop to logging what is happening there.

The "how" of field note-taking requires a good deal of flexibility and sensitivity to the situation. Given the frailties of human memory, it is always better to log observations sooner rather than later (at least within 24 hours). This is easier in busy public spaces where one can remain relatively inconspicuous while jotting in a notebook. But there are many occasions when writing notes would intrude on the natural course of events and even give offense. For these occastions, Lofland and Lofland (1995) describe a sequence of taking mental notes—committing to memory as much as possible—followed by brief jottings or speaking into a tape recorder (retreating to the bathroom is a favorite technique for accomplishing this). At the end of the day, write in greater detail what was seen. Psychological experiments on human memory show that waiting more than a day can seriously erode one's recall.

Field note-taking can be time consuming and divert one from actual observation (Agar, 1980). As with all of ethnography, fieldnotes have been targeted by critics who question their presumed objectivity (Atkinson & Hammersley, 1994; Van Maanen, 1988). Questions about the nature of ethnographic representation are understandable, and we should be careful not to overstate the value of our fieldnotes. Yet pragmatism must prevail. Conceding that all observation is refracted through one or more lenses, we must push on and take thorough fieldnotes as best we can.

Lofland and Lofland (1995, pp. 89-98) provide helpful hints for field note-taking:

1. Aim for the concrete and specific in describing behaviors and events. At the beginning, try to avoid any inferences, whether your own or volunteered by those you are observing.

2. Try to distinguish between the different types or levels of observational data based on their proximity to the event being observed. First-order data such as verbatim accounts are recorded either during, or immediately after, the period of observation. The second level of data involves paraphrasing of conversations and less certain recall after observation has taken place. Ideas regarding new directions and inferences are further along the continuum of removal from the event and are periodically recorded in *analytic memos.* The final level of abstraction, *concept development and theory generation,* involves generating a meaningful explanatory framework that has been developed from ground level up.

3. Record observations of yourself—your impressions, feelings, and concerns. You can bracket this information in your fieldnotes or log it separately in a diary. Keeping a running commentary of personal reactions and feelings serves two related purposes. First, it is an outlet—a place to unload the inevitably human reactions to prolonged contact with others. Second, it provides a means of identifying personal biases and devising ways to manage them.

4. Strive for balance—don't let yourself become lost in a forest of minutiae, yet don't lose the tendency to compulsiveness that motivates

the best field observers. Even small amounts of time spent in the field translate into lengthy notes. The ratio is around 6 to 1—6 hours of recording for every hour of observation (Agar, 1980).

The average field notebook does not read like pulp fiction—it may seem overlong and tedious to an outside reader. At times, the burden to record as much as possible can be onerous; most ethnographers have at least one story of hiding from an informant to avoid yet another noteworthy encounter. A 15-minute chat might require an hour or more of write-up!

Nevertheless, the only way to make sure that you do not miss anything is to be a bit compulsive, at least at first. Later, you will be able to develop your own regimen of recording and memoing that is focused and productive.

INTENSIVE INTERVIEWING

It is a natural segue from field observation, where one engages in informal questioning of informants, to data collection by formal interview. Unlike on-the-spot interviewing during field observation, intensive interviewing is scheduled in advance, takes place in a setting conducive to conversation and candor, and requires some preparation.

But there is a good deal of variation in how an intensive interview is planned and how it unfolds. No matter how well planned, an interview can seem like "taking a puppy for a walk" (Steinmetz, 1991, p. 64). An interviewer who is patient and flexible can usually get the puppy to "heel" in time.

A Few Guidelines for Starting Out

A qualitative interview is a goal-directed conversation. It should not be confused with a clinical or therapeutic interview. Nor should it be considered unstructured or unfocused, subject to the whims of its participants. Good qualitative interviewers have skills that are honed from trial-and-error experience in the field.

A few helpful hints come in handy when contemplating qualitative interviewing. These are drawn from the works of several seasoned qualitative researchers, including Robert Weiss (1994), Margot Ely et al. (1991), and John and Lyn Lofland (1995). We start with broader issues and become more concrete as we go along.

First, clarify your *stance* as much as possible, situating it along a detachment-attachment continuum. Although all informants are encouraged to see the interviewer as an eager, uninformed learner, the interviewer provides gentle guidance and directs the flow of the interview. It may be a partnership, but the roles are different and complementary. Part of the interviewer stance involves deciding how much to engage in repartee with one's informants. The nature of the interviewing relationship opens the door to expressions of concern and personal self-disclosure by the interviewer. A judicious amount of "joining" with one's informants facilitates disclosure and makes an interview more conversational and free flowing.

Second, develop an *interview guide* beforehand and pilot test it on a few persons before actual data collection begins. An interview guide should contain an initial set of questions that focus on your areas of interest. The guide should provide enough detail to cover key domains, but should not become a straitjacket.

Some qualitative researchers reject using questions developed beforehand. In his book on homeless women, Eliot Liebow (1993) explained his approach to interviewing:

> I was under no pressure to bring ready-made questions into the study situation. I did ask questions, of course, but these were not questions I brought with me from the outside. They are "natural" questions that arose spontaneously and directly out of social situations. . . . They were situation-specific questions, not research questions. (p. 321)

Novice qualitative researchers (and researchers writing formal grant proposals) may want to forego following Liebow's hang-loose approach. Although the respondent's story is always more important than a rigid interview guide, most qualitative researchers come prepared.

Questions should not be phrased to lead respondents toward a particular answer or emotional state. Of course, once a respondent mentions that an event or person was upsetting, the door is open for the interviewer to follow up. Good qualitative interviewers learn to make use of *probes,* questions used to go deeper to pursue leads wittingly or unwittingly provided by informants.

Some of the most valuable information in qualitative interviews emerges from spontaneous probes; it is here that the interviewer must remain alert and open minded. Recognizing a lead, the interviewer may say, "you mentioned _____ earlier; could you tell me more about that?" In our

Mammogram Study, we queried respondents regarding their beliefs about what caused breast cancer to spread in the body and several mentioned their belief that "air" is responsible. Intrigued, our interviewers probed further. Respondents explained that opening up the body during surgery exposed "dormant" cancer cells to the air and precipitated their spread throughout the body. Clearly, this kind of unsolicited information could shed light on why women do (or do not) follow up clinical recommendations for surgical biopsies and other diagnostic services.

Lofland and Lofland (1995) recommend appending *facesheets* and *interviewer reaction sheets* to the interview guide. The *facesheet* is a standardized document for recording the date, time, and location of the interview as well as the demographic characteristics (age, sex, race or ethnicity, etc.) of the informant. The *interviewer reaction sheet* is a place to log observations about the interviewee (the informant seemed hostile, distracted, overly eager to please, etc.) and about the setting (the inform-ant's home was immaculately kept, the clinic waiting room was chaotic, etc.). It is also a good idea to jot down personal reactions to the interview, your concerns and feelings, as well as ideas to follow up.

One of my former doctoral students, Susan Letteney, kindly agreed to share the following excerpt from her journal, written after interviewing the daughter of a gay parent:

> I find that the impulse to jump in, interpret, clarify . . . are natural responses for me. . . . It is here that my experience as a clinician serves as an obstacle. . . . If I wait, sit on my impulses, the subject answers my questions and more. She finds meaning and clarification in her own way. . . . I also learned about myself as an interviewer. Not a comfortable role. Actually, the aspect of asking questions and exploring was quite comfortable. Sitting quietly, not responding, was alien. I asked fewer questions than I would have liked, to get used to the idea of listening more and interacting less. I also did not want to contaminate the interview with leading questions.

It is difficult to overstate the importance of observational data as a crucial adjunct to interview data. Even the most meticulous transcript of the interview leaves out vital information. Tone of voice, affective expres-sions (sighs, sobs, laughs), body language, and the ambience of the setting (noise, interruptions by others) all provide a feeling for the context that enriches and informs.

A final guideline is to build into the study ways to elicit and enhance *rapport*. For example, you may consider beginning and ending the interview with "feel-good" questions. Such questions can be of the "tell me about your typical day" variety designed to put informants at ease and remind them that a qualitative research interview is more like a conversation than an inquisition.

Common Problems in Qualitative Interviewing

Even veteran qualitative researchers have had that sinking experience of an interview gone awry—the "taking a puppy for a walk" feeling. Losing control of an interview leads to frustration and self-doubt. But it need not (and should not) happen often.

It helps if one can anticipate some of the common pitfalls of qualitative interviewing. One pitfall occurs when the desire to control or lead compels the interviewer to stop listening and to cut off or interrupt the informant. Another difficulty occurs when the interview lacks "flow." Conducting an interview is akin to floating gently down a stream. A skilled interviewer can adroitly manuever around the obstacles and keep things flowing along. Topics segue smoothly into one another and probes are used when appropriate.

Then there are those occasions when *narrative flow* is elusive or impossible. It is frustrating to sit across from a cryptic informant who answers questions in monosyllables, then sits impassively waiting for the next question. The interview stops and starts, frustrations rise, and the interviewer feels at wit's end.

Uncooperative informants can be one of the most exasperating experiences a qualitative researcher will have. A suspicious executive, a sullen adolescent, or a harried parent may be evasive during the interview and even sabotage it so that it will end. Qualitative researchers know it is not a matter of if, but when, this will happen. The best tactic in these situations is to remain calm, be diplomatic, and withdraw when necessary. No amount of information is worth risking coercion (or a migraine headache).

During the ebb and flow of a successful interview, qualitative researchers strike a balance between the general and the particular, the need to stay focused versus the need to probe deeper. This is a juggling act that takes time and skill to pull off. A successful interview is one in which the interviewer has elicited valuable information by observing, listening, probing, and synthesizing information on the spot when necessary. The back and forth of the conversation is not aimless, but proceeds with direction. When everything has clicked, both interviewer and interviewee part company feeling they have had a mutually beneficial encounter.

Emotional Issues in Interviewing

The sensitive and probing nature of qualitative research almost guarantees that emotionally laden information will surface. Informants may laugh, sob, or grow angry during an interview. Because the vast majority of informants welcome the opportunity to tell their story to an empathic, nonjudgmental listener, it is rare that emotions cause more than momentary interruptions.

Human subjects committees sometimes protest that studies of sensitive topics can set off a chain reaction of emotional turmoil and harm research participants. But Weiss (1994) argued that the nature of qualitative interviewing mitigates against this. Even when interviews prompt strong emotional reactions, a skilled interviewer can show concern and then gently steer respondents from stormy to calmer seas.

In any event, the qualitative interviewer never tries to elicit strong emotions, only to create a safe space for their expression, should they occur. Even short-term emotional harm is unlikely in the vast majority of qualitative studies.

Social work researchers have reason to be concerned about emotional issues because our informants often come from troubled backgrounds and live troubled lives. We need not avoid expressing humane concern and empathy during an interview. However, the social work researcher should avoid assuming the stance of a clinician *or* friend. When assistance is requested or needed, referrals for counseling or services can be made at the end of the interview.

What is often overlooked in qualitative research are the effects on the interviewer—the backwash of emotions that follows an intense, long interview. From the informant's perspective, the experience is usually one of catharsis and good will—many express satisfaction and volunteer to meet again. The interviewer's reactions may be more varied. Satisfaction may be tempered by exhaustion and numbness. Unlike the relationship between clinician and client, the research interviewer does not have the protection of clinical distance, settling instead for the "emotional middle distance" (Weiss, 1994, p. 123).

Focus-Group Interviewing

Most qualitative researchers pursue interviewing as a one-to-one activity, but group interviews can also be useful because they draw on a form of synergy between group members. Although the term "focus group" originated in sociology (Merton, Fiske, & Kendall, 1956), its application has become most common in marketing and polling surveys, where small groups of unrelated individuals are brought together to discuss a new product or political candidate (Greenbaum, 1993; Morgan, 1988).

The size of a focus group should be large enough to generate diversity of opinions, but small enough to allow everyone to share in the discussion—about 7 to 10 is optimal (Krueger, 1994). Ideally, the focus group is composed of persons from similar backgrounds who do not know each other very well. Familiarity among group members can lead to more habitual ways of interacting and inhibit "fresh" opinions from emerging.

Especially problematic are focus groups composed of family members or persons from different levels of a status hierarchy, especially bosses and their underlings. Married couples or parents and adult children can bring too much emotional baggage into the group to allow free discourse. Similarly, subordinates in a work organization are not likely to feel at liberty to speak their mind with their bosses present. It makes more sense to convene focus groups of staff from within the various levels of the organization hierarchy or to go to one-on-one interviewing.

Focus-group interviewing typically involves a group leader who asks open-ended questions, but the degree of direction and structure can vary depending on how narrow or broad is the topic of inquiry. In addition to the need to be sensitive, flexible, and empathic, the group leader must avoid certain pitfalls common to group situations (Fontana & Frey, 1994). These include domination by one person or a clique and lack of participation by some group members. Poor group leaders—those who dominate the discussion or are too passive—can make focus groups a disaster. But even good focus-group leaders can find it difficult to facilitate an open discussion and to channel members away from internal dissension or from diversionary tactics like bullying and ridicule. When the topic being discussed is volatile, the risks are obviously even greater.

Focus-group interviewing brings some clear advantages to a qualitative study, including savings in time and resources and the elicitation of rich qualitative data from individuals stimulated by a group format. Focus-group interviewing in social work research is particularly well suited to studies of organizations and of professional issues in settings where there is a web of social networks already in place. It is far easier to conduct focus groups whose members have shared interests than to convince a group of total strangers to attend a group interview. Focus groups can be useful in conducting needs assessment, in studies of organizational change, and in learning about what clients or staff think about certain policies or practices.

But focus groups also have their limitations. First, they are better suited for eliciting opinions than personal stories—they are *not* group-therapy sessions. For many highly sensitive topics, focus groups are simply not suitable. It is not difficult to think of issues in social work research that are best dealt with by one-on-one interviewing.

Second, focus-group interviewing takes an enormous amount of patience and skill. A focus group can be multiply exasperating if participants are uncooperative, an experience akin to trying to herd cats. Participants who will not accept the ground rules of the group interview can make it difficult for those who do. Even the logistics—finding a comfortable place to convene and getting everyone to show up—can be daunting in this era of busy schedules.

Despite these drawbacks, focus-group interviewing has become an important means of data collection, especially in studies of organizations and in program evaluation. When used appropriately, they are an efficient and effective way to collect interview data.

Matching Interviewers to Respondents: Pros and Cons

As mentioned in Chapter 2, the decision to *match* interviewers to respondents by sex, ethnicity, or other criteria is not an easy one. Beyond the obvious need to match by language, there are no set rules to follow. When interviewer and respondent are of the same sex or race, understanding is enhanced and certain topics can be more freely addressed.

But matching can also introduce problems arising from misplaced assumptions. Teri Friedman (1991), in her study of female police officers, was delighted and a bit relieved to interview an officer who shared her Jewish ethnic identity. But after some initial banter about Yiddish and kosher diets, she found that their social-class backgrounds differed so much that they had nothing else in common.

Once matching begins, how far does one go? Shared gender, for example, may not be enough to bridge the gap between a white middle-class researcher and a homeless Puerto Rican mother. Further, it is not easy to anticipate which interviewer characteristics will help or hinder a study. Robert Weiss (1994) noted,

> When I interviewed men who were IV drug users, I was an outsider to the drug culture but an insider to the world of men. When I interviewed a woman who was an IV drug user living in a shelter and also the mother of two children, I was an outsider to the world of women, drug users, and women's shelters, but an insider to the concerns of parents. (p. 137)

Using "indigenous" members of the community as interviewers is often useful but also carries some risks. Respondents may fear a loss of privacy by speaking to "one of their own" or they may slant their responses to avoid loss of face with a compatriot. They may feel resentful and competitive or try to ingratiate themselves and give socially desirable answers to questions.

For some studies, the effectiveness of the interview may depend on matching; for others, a skilled interviewer is sufficient. A good dose of common sense should guide decisions about the most appropriate type of person to collect data.

Use of Audiotapes and Videotapes and Other Logistical Considerations

You are probably well aware by now how labor-intensive and low-tech qualitative research is. Anyone with the proper training can enter the field with only a notebook and a keen sense of curiosity about people. There are, however, technological accoutrements such as audiotape and videotape recorders and computers that greatly enhance data collection. A laptop computer might, for example, be used for notetaking in the field.

For researchers able to afford and operate the equipment, videotaping can provide valuable documentation of verbal and nonverbal behavior for later analysis. Like any form of observation, videotapes are selective representations and should not be construed as the "whole picture." The presence of video recorders may distort behaviors and give a false impression of naturalism. Despite these caveats, many qualitative researchers favor videotaping to supplement other forms of data collection.

Audiotaping interviews is becoming commonplace these days. The intrepid qualitative interviewer sallies forth equipped with extra tapes and batteries, determined to capture all of the nuances of voice and sound. Although some informants may refuse permission for taping (necessitating the more intrusive alternative of notetaking), most accept the tape recorder and soon forget that it is being used.

Audiotaping allows the interviewer to concentrate on what is being said (although briefly jotting down major points and observations to supplement the taping is not a bad idea). It is also more inclusive than notetaking. Audiotapes capture laughter, sighs, sarcasm—aspects of the interview that are vivid and revealing.

Other logistical concerns relate to the timing, length, and setting of the interview. Given the balance of power in the researcher-respondent relationship, qualitative researchers must maintain flexible schedules, remain alert when respondents feel like talking for hours, and be prepared to conduct interviews in some very unusual places. Some interview settings tax the patience of even the most dedicated researcher—crying children, complaining spouses, ringing telephones, and other ambient noise may be too distracting to overcome. The best response on these occasions is to push on (if the respondent is willing) and reschedule if necessary.

USING DOCUMENTS
AND EXISTING DATA

A variety of documents and archival materials are available to social work researchers: court records, case reports, minutes of meetings, agency brochures, transcripts, census data, diaries, letters, and so forth. Recently, computer mavens have used electronic media such as e-mail and the Internet as sources of research data (Workman, 1992). Whereas historiographers typically focus on archival materials as their primary source of data, most qualitative researchers use documents to supplement data from interviewing and observation.

The least obtrusive type of data, documents can provide valuable information on the lives of individuals, on the history of an important social agency or institution, or even on broad social trends. The approach used to analyze documents, known as *content analysis,* is not exclusive to qualitative research and has its own history of development in conjunction with quantitative studies (Berelson, 1952). Qualitative researchers may also report numbers, percents, or frequencies from content analyses of documents, but they usually treat documents as raw data much like interview transcripts or fieldnotes.

In addition to documents, existing data sets from earlier research studies may be available for qualitative analyses. Many psychotherapy training institutes maintain archives of videotapes and audiotapes of psychotherapy sessions for training and research purposes. Similarly, qualitative researchers often have an abundance of data that they are willing to loan for secondary analyses.

In contrast to existing data, documents have some disadvantages because they were not produced for research purposes. They may be inaccurate, uneven, and incomplete. (Agency case records and hospital medical charts are among the worst offenders here.) Some of this is due to hurried record keeping but sometimes it is deliberate. For example, minutes of meetings may be "doctored" to cover up embarrassing revelations about an organization, or a physician may omit mention of a mental problem in a medical file to protect her patient from stigma. Obviously, a study dependent on documents and existing research data is constrained by what is available and its quality.

ADVANTAGES AND DISADVANTAGES OF VARIOUS TYPES OF DATA COLLECTION

For all of their potential flaws, documents and existing data have one clear advantage over interviewing and observation—their lack of *reactivity*. In contrast, the presence of an ethnographic observer or an interviewer has an obvious impact on the natural course of events no matter how unobtrusive one tries to be. Use of documents is usually less time consuming and always less emotionally taxing when compared to observation and interviewing.

Yet observation and interviewing afford the unique opportunity to produce the kind of data that make qualitative studies so memorable and valued. Analyses of existing data cannot provide the warmth and good cheer that follow a successful interview or day in the field. In addition, observation and interviewing give the researcher far more control over what, how, and when data are produced. The nature of the data—their firm grounding in the real world of respondents—is worth the risk of reactivity.

Of course, all forms of empirical data are filtered in some way, whether by a clinician or by a field observer—the lens may grossly distort or only slightly refract. Observation and interviewing in qualitative research do have one advantage over existing data—their conduct allows the deployment of safeguards to minimize distortion. As we will see in Chapter 8, qualitative researchers need not throw up their hands when it comes to issues of bias.

ENDING DATA COLLECTION AND LEAVING THE FIELD

Thus far, we have discussed several types of qualitative data: fieldnotes, audiotapes and videotapes, logs or diaries, transcripts of interviews, and documents. Although a detailed discussion of data analysis is reserved for the next chapter, data analysis should begin as soon as possible after data collection has begun, thereby guiding data collection as the study proceeds.

The decision to stop data collection depends not on quantity so much as quality. Notwithstanding the desire we all have for certainty and predictability, there are no hard and fast rules about when to quit collecting data. When one has achieved *saturation* in data collection—when additional observation, interviews, and documents become redundant and reveal no new information—then data collection can end.

Whereas one might think that ending data collection is a source of great relief, many a qualitative researcher has postponed the inevitable. Sometimes we are reluctant to leave our informants behind, assuming that they need us (an assumption more comforting than true in most cases). At times, we have become so attached to our respondents that separation anxieties paralyze us. Then there are those of us who wish to postpone the moment of truth when we must face the data and make sense of it. In this context, we look back fondly on the "good old days" of data collection and cast a weary eye at the boxes (or diskettes) of data waiting for attention.

Two aspects of data collection are distinct in qualitative research—the flexibility of the time frame and the likelihood of return visits to the field. Just as a baseball game is played until finished (unlike football or basketball, where a clock ticks away), there is no set time limit to qualitative research.

Anthropologists have a tradition of staying one or more years in the field to capture the complete annual cycle of events among the people they are studying. Although this may seem impossibly long to the average social work researcher (who must balance fieldwork with other responsibilities), qualitative research does require large blocks of time to achieve immersion and engagement.

The need for prolonged engagement also typically leads to more than one meeting with an informant to retrieve new information, check codes and interpretations, and share the study's findings. Ely et al. (1991) recommend keeping the door open when leaving informants, keeping an understanding that a follow-up interview or phone call may be needed. This makes leaving the field a bit easier for both parties because closure is not final. Many qualitative researchers maintain contacts with their informants long after the study has ended.

SUMMARY AND CONCLUSION

This chapter provided a description of the three main types of data collection in qualitative research: observation, interviewing, and document review. To offset the advantages and disadvantages of each, qualitative researchers typically collect more than one type of data.

Most qualitative studies include the unbeatable combination of interviewing and observation. Although it is possible to conduct a purely observational study (unobtrusive observation) or a purely archival study (historiography), one cannot (and should not) collect interview data without also carrying out observation when carrying out a full-scale qualitative study. Observations of the interviewee, the setting, the larger context, and (last but not least) ourselves give much-needed breadth and depth to interview data.

CODA: A FEW EXERCISES IN QUALITATIVE DATA COLLECTION TO GET YOUR FEET WET

The following exercises introduce some of the basics of qualitative data collection and are relatively easy to do.

Exercise 1: An Hour in the Life . . .

Spend an hour or more in the "field" as an ethnographer. This may be in a park, playground, cafe, subway station, or sports arena—any public space where behavior can be unobtrusively observed. As you carry out your observations, take in-depth field notes. Report on the physical space, the actors, the behaviors, the emotions expressed, and the ambience of the setting (time of day, unusual events, etc.). After your fieldnotes are written up, scrutinize them closely (or show them to a colleague) and place brackets around portions that appear more interpretive than descriptive. In other words, try to separate straightforward reporting from your assumptions or biases.

Exercise 2: Shadowing

"Shadowing" refers to getting permission to follow a person around during his or her daily activities to observe and take notes (Ely et al., 1991). The goal is to enter that person's world as much as possible without being intrusive. Depending on the focus of your study (and the willingness of your respondent), you might shadow an agency supervisor, a troubled adolescent, a single parent, or a drug dealer.

Exercise 3: Learning about the Rashomon Effect

My colleague Dr. Carla Mariano (an Associate Professor of Nursing at New York University) suggests using this classroom exercise: Show a movie or video with the sound turned off and ask students to comment on what they see. This can demonstrate how easily multiple interpretations of the same event can emerge, similar to the Japanese movie *Rashomon*, where a single event was recounted in as many ways as there were observers.

Exercise 4: Memory Fails . . .

This exercise is designed to impress upon students the need to take fieldnotes either during or immediately after the observed event. Students are asked to think about some discrete event they recently experienced—going to a movie, attending a ballgame or a wedding, and so forth. They are asked to write down a full description of the event—who was there, what happened, what the setting looked like, and the like. This experience invariably illustrates the fragility of memory.

Exercise 5: Conducting an Interview

Students are asked to focus on a topic of interest and seek out a knowledgeable respondent for an open-ended interview. The interview is audiotaped and transcribed and excerpts are shared in class. This exercise exposes the student to the intensity and flexibility of a qualitative interview. It also illustrates graphically how time-consuming interviewing and transcribing are!

Chapter 7

DATA MANAGEMENT AND ANALYSIS

As the data begin to accumulate, the qualitative researcher confronts a new challenge. If data collection can be said to draw on social skills, data management and analysis are relatively solitary, cerebral pursuits. They test the researcher's ability to think creatively and conceptually. Unlike quantitative research, where a well-trained assistant may assume many of the tasks of data management and analysis, the qualitative researcher is the instrument of data collection *and* analysis.

As much as I hope this chapter will provide some helpful suggestions, no textbook can substitute for learning by doing (and by trial and error). Many a qualitative researcher contemplating data analysis looks back fondly to fieldwork as an idyllic period. A few become overwhelmed by the analysis phase—thereby entering the Bermuda Triangle of qualitative research never to be heard from again.

But the intrepid researcher should take heart. Despite its demands, qualitative data analysis can also be an exciting time for creativity and improvisation. When findings begin to emerge, the sense of accomplishment—of producing new knowledge—is immensely gratifying.

LEVELS OF QUALITATIVE DATA—
FROM THE RAW TO THE COOKED

Huberman and Miles (1994) offered a hierarchical typology of qualitative data based on the degree of abstraction and processing ("cooking") of the data. Thus, *raw data* include tapes, fieldnotes, and documents and *partially processed data* include transcripts and logged comments by the researcher. The next level of data is *codes* or categories—abstracted *meaning units* drawn from raw and partially processed data. Also generated at this stage are *analytic memos* (explaining the decision making behind the codes).

The researcher may wish to use *graphic displays* such as charts, matrices, and maps to diagram social networks, physical settings and their layout, or relations between codes or concepts in the study. You may also choose to compile *case studies or vignettes* to illustrate categories or themes. All along the transition from raw to cooked, the researcher is maintaining an indexing system for storage and retrieval, documenting analytic decisions in a log, and using a journal or diary to record personal observations and experiences in the field.

The diversity of approaches to data management and analysis in qualitative research reflects the multiple epistemological stances of its "donor" disciplines (McCracken, 1988). Sociology produced the systematic approach of grounded theory complete with methodological terms such as open coding, axial coding, and conditional matrices (Glaser, 1992; Strauss & Corbin, 1990). At the other end of the continuum, anthropologists favor a less prescriptive and less formal tradition (Agar, 1991). The absence of a formalized methodology has given the field of anthropology—the pioneering donor discipline—a low profile in the qualitative methods literature. For many anthropologists, a methods course would take away too much of the mystique of the field.

Regardless of disciplinary influence, data analytic techniques in qualitative research are *inductive*—moving from the specific to the general—and *systematic.* Contrary to prevailing myths among the uninformed, qualitative data analysis is neither haphazard nor a product of the researcher's whims. Creativity need not detract from rigor.

One of the primary criticisms of quantitative studies is that they are reductionistic. But qualitative studies are also reductionistic in their own way. The difference? Quantitative research prescribes data reduction *before* data collection begins and qualitative researchers reduce data *after* they are collected. Quantitative researchers pride themselves on giving their readers a detailed description of the variables, measures, and data-analytic procedures used in their study. Although not exactly scintillating reading, these explications of method provide a necessary backdrop to interpreting the findings (and ultimately replicating them).

Few qualitative studies offer comparable details on their analytic procedures. Some qualitative researchers even object to such documentation, saying it interferes with creativity and spontaneity. Qualitative reports are usually a good read, but they too often rest on a foundation of the unknown. This need not be the case.

In this chapter, I will provide some general guidelines common to most qualitative studies and discuss the various techniques employed to manage and analyze data, including use of computers. Regardless of the techniques or interpretive lenses you decide to use, you will need to start the journey by organizing your data.

DATA MANAGEMENT:
DEALING WITH VOLUME EARLY ON

Even experienced qualitative researchers are surprised by the sheer quantity of raw data generated by studying "only a few" people. Most qualitative researchers find themselves inundated with boxes of files, tapes, notebooks, and computer diskettes after leaving the field. Manwar and colleagues (1994) studied 80 crack dealers in New York City and generated more than 25,000 pages of textual data! A case study of the life of an individual (or of an agency, a family, or small town) can generate similar quantities of data. Given the approximate 6 to 1 ratio of time spent organizing and analyzing data versus time in the field, one can only wonder when and where it will all end.

By comparison, quantitative studies yield precoded numerical data that are entered into a computerized file and "cooked" (analyzed) following the standard recipes. Data management consists largely of cleaning the data (correcting entry errors) and creating datasets for analysis—a far cry from the tasks facing the qualitative researcher.

Sue Estroff (1981) described a typical approach to data management that she used in her own ethnographic work:

> When I refer to data, I mean primarily volumes of field notes filled with verbatim and reconstructed conversations, my own thoughts and feelings, descriptions of events and individual behaviors, synopses of discussions, and miscellaneous information collected from a variety of sources. The other materials I used were notes made by clients (some solicited and some unsolicited) and staff, CAS (Community Adaptation Schedule) responses that were computed, coded, and scored, some transcribed tapes of in-depth interviews with staff members, and veritable mountains of newspaper clippings,

books, and scholarly articles. I created a file for each client that contained essential information such as demographic, admission, and discharge facts. In addition, these files contained medication, employment, and personal histories as well as current status—all as reported to me by the clients. (p. 33)

She goes on to vividly describe her hands-on approach to data analysis:

Working with these materials was a messy, exasperating, and complicated procedure. I began by reading all the field notes and raw materials repeatedly until I knew what was in each volume and where it was, creating a sort of mental map and table of contents. Then, as the structure and order of presentation of topics became clearer, I literally surrounded myself with data. I made concentric circles of important pages of field notes, articles, books, and drafts, and I perched in the middle of these to think, sort, and combine. Each of these circles became a chapter, but only after it had become a shambles. Days were spent shuffling and grabbing, realizing a whole section needed rewriting and so beginning again, or rescuing all from numerous disasters with the paws of muddy dogs who assaulted me for attention. (pp. 33-34)

The goal of qualitative data management is to organize and store data for maximal efficiency in retrieval and analysis. A good first step in data management occurs throughout data collection: All fieldnotes, interview notes, diaries, and memos should have the date, time, and place recorded on each entry. In addition to filing by topic and by data type, you may wish to keep a file on each respondent. Protecting confidentiality of informants should be of paramount concern—use of a code number or pseudonym in the data allows the person's identity to be known only to the researcher.

TRANSCRIBING
AUDIOTAPED INTERVIEWS

Transcription of audiotapes should begin early. If you are a one-person operation, you will do this yourself. If you have a professional transcriber, this can be expensive but it saves enormous amounts of time (transcribing a 2-hour interview can take up to 10 hours and produce 30 or more pages of transcription). On the other hand, there is no greater intimacy with interview data than that gained from transcribing your own tapes. In addition to getting closer to the data, it affords an opportunity for immediate feedback on your performance as an interviewer—opening the door to making improvements in your interviewing technique.

In either case, it is useful to develop some basic rules for transcription and ensure that they are followed consistently. These include rules for transcribing vocal utterances such as sighs, sobs, or laughter. Pauses by the respondent lasting more than a few seconds may be worth noting in the transcript. Finally, the transcriber should strive to capture every word verbatim—no matter how poorly these words come across. As anyone who transcribes an audiotape realizes, speech is often messy when put into print. But respondents have a right to have their stories transcribed verbatim without cosmetic (and potentially distorting) revisions.

As the typewriter has become a relic of the past, you will likely use a computer word-processing program for transcribing data. Your task will be enhanced considerably if you leave ample margins (for notations) and number the lines (for later coding). One ironclad rule: Make back-up copies of all work whether on computer diskettes or hard copies. Although some variant of this story has made the rounds among many doctoral students, I once knew a doctoral student who experienced the ultimate nightmare— she returned from the field only to have all of her data stolen from the trunk of her car with no copies stored elsewhere!

CODING THE DATA:
THE SEARCH FOR MEANING

There is no single approach to qualitative data analysis; qualitative researchers tend to pursue what works best given the data at hand. Many qualitative researchers begin with *line-by-line coding*. Coding qualitative data is a process of identifying bits and pieces of information (*meaning units*) and linking these to *concepts and themes* around which the final report is organized. In the spirit of inductive inquiry, the researcher begins at the most basic level—reading and rereading every line of text in the search for meaning units.

At this stage, it is best to use "open coding" (Emerson, Fretz, & Shaw, 1995) and resist the temptation to rely on a priori concepts to understand the data. For example, if you are studying terminally ill patients, you may be tempted to recall Kubler-Ross's (1969) stages of acceptance of death as you attempt to make sense of their experience. Or perhaps you are studying adolescent girls with eating disorders and you rely on Margaret Mahler's theory of separation-individuation as a way of understanding their condition. In these instances, the use of preexisting concepts tends to obscure more than enlighten. If taken too far, the data become subordinate and induction becomes deduction.

The open-ended approach is a bit anxiety provoking to the researcher who is unaccustomed to it. It is also time consuming and painstaking in the beginning. But once mastered, open coding becomes almost second nature. Reading a transcript, I cannot resist the urge to use the margins to note ideas and potential themes. These ideas form a fragile web that is either strengthened by later coding or revised to fit the data.

Coding decisions should be documented by *memoing* so that they may be scrutinized later by the researcher or by an auditor (a process described in more detail in Chapter 8). Memos put into writing the researcher's thoughts and ideas about what is going on in the data (Emerson, Fretz, & Shaw, 1995). As coding proceeds, we separate the wheat from the chaff, knowing that there is far more data than we need, yet not knowing what is discardable until all data have been analyzed. This act of diving into the data takes as much persistence as insight. I have read portions of a transcript that seemed uninteresting initially, then marvelled at my lack of attention upon a second (or third) reading. Some bits of information become meaning units after a conceptual framework begins to take shape. What is important is that you get to know your data well enough to know where the treasures are.

One of the most commonly used methods of coding is *constant comparative analysis,* a technique associated with *grounded theory* (Strauss & Corbin, 1990). In practice, it is iterative, beginning as inductive, then becoming deductive, then returning to an inductive approach. As themes emerge from initial coding (inductive phase), one goes back over the data to ensure that it is coded in accordance with these themes (deductive phase). As one combs back through the data, new codes often emerge (inductive phase).

If, for example, you develop a code or category midway through analyzing transcripts, you may need to return to earlier transcripts to see if it is present. In this manner, one examines the data, first with a fine-toothed comb, then moves on to higher levels of abstraction as a categorical schema begins to fall into place.

Table 7.1 illustrates the iterative nature of coding by presenting two consecutive versions of categories that emerged from our initial coding of transcripts in the Mammogram Study. Four members of our research team coded the same transcripts independently, then met to compare our coding and develop a consensus list of categories.

Table 7.1

Example of Two Iterations of Coding
Categories From the Mammogram Study*

Version 1	Version 2
Why Mammogram	Why Mammogram
Why Site	Why Site
Satisfaction With Information	Satisfaction With Information
Mammogram Results	Mammogram Results
Previous Experience With Mammography	Previous Experience With Mammography
Plans for Future Breast Care	Plans for Future Breast Care
Causes of Breast Cancer	*Why Follow-Up (After Abnormal Mammogram)*
Why Cancer Spreads	Causes of Breast Cancer
Breast Cancer and Sexuality	Why Cancer Spreads
Evaluation of Doctors/Nurses	Breast Cancer and Sexuality
Evaluation of Site	*Cancer Fears*
Choice of Doctor	Evaluation of Doctors/Nurses
Race and Health Care	Evaluation of Site
Financial Issues	Choice of Doctor
Taking Care of Health	Race and Health Care
Advice to Other Women	Financial Issues
	System Problems/Barriers
	Taking Care of Health/*Help Seeking*
	Other Health Problems
	Advice to Other Women
	Religion/Spirituality

*Changes shown in italics.

As shown in Table 7.1, the initial coding of transcripts yielded several categories related to the women's experiences with mammography and their concerns about health care, breast cancer, race, and so forth. In the second iteration, several new categories were added and one category renamed. For example, the added category "other health problems" was derived from references to diabetes, hypertension, and other medical conditions that emerged from the second set of transcripts that we coded.

We reasoned that health problems might interfere with (or delay) their decision about follow-up after an abnormal mammogram and agreed that such information should be coded and retrievable. The category "taking care of health" was later renamed "taking care of health/help-seeking" after a lengthy discussion about how best to capture both the self-help philosophy espoused by many of the women as well as their assertiveness in seeking help from medical providers.

As the coded excerpts accumulate, subcategories may be necessary. For example, "causes of breast cancer" can be further classified into diet, genetic predisposition, environment, and so forth. Similarly, the code "why site" will most probably yield several reasons for why the respondents chose a particular mammography clinic—for example, affordable, close to home, or convenient hours. As categories and subcategories unfold in the Mammogram Study, we will continue to refine our concepts and return to the data to verify them.

How do we know when to stop? Coding draws to a close when we begin to see repetition and redundancy—new information tends to confirm our existing classification scheme and discrepant cases stop appearing. This state of grace is known as *saturation,* a term meaning the "cooking" process is drawing to an end.

Table 7.2 offers a sampling of excerpts from the transcripts that are linked to specific codes. Each excerpt has a parentheses enclosing the identification number for the respondent and the line numbers from the transcript (so that the excerpt's origins can be easily traced). It should be noted that, just as one category will most likely be linked to several excerpts, a single excerpt may fit into more than one category. For example, one of our respondents reported feeling fearful and anxious about losing her sexual attractiveness if she had a mastectomy. This excerpt would be placed under two codes—"breast cancer and sexuality" and "cancer fears."

It is not necessary for all or even most respondents to adhere to a particular code. At times, even a single event or case is so instructive that we report it. We need not fear reporting only one example of some incident or behavior (or only one case associated with a particular category) as long as we are candid about its singularity. Of course, we take heart when something occurs with frequency, as an argument may be strengthened by numbers.

Outliers usually spell trouble in a statistical analysis (they may even be deleted to "normalize" the distribution), but they matter in qualitative research. Deviant cases bring into sharper relief the very norms they flout.

Table 7.2

Examples of Coded Excerpts From the Mammogram Study*

Category	Excerpts
Causes of Breast Cancer	"I would say, actually it's what you ingest, . . . what you eat." (246:347-349)
	". . . sometimes the radiation gives the cancer . . . or it's in the genes." (024:365-66)
	"The ones who smoke . . . maybe how many children you have, maybe if you breast-fed. I think the more children you have, the less likely you should (have breast cancer)." (192:127-130)
	"[My] sister got hit in the back . . . it was years ago and during that time they didn't know nothing about cancer. And the doctor operated on her, [he] said it was a wind she had in her back . . . and then I had to take her to another place 20 miles away and that's when they discovered she had cancer." (251:560-566)
Why Cancer Spreads	"Well I think from the calcium buildup, sometimes you have, it spreads out, like a lump or something, like the root of a tree. And it has those little roots, just the cells." (024:258-269)
	". . . I've been told that once the air hits, if it's severe enough, it will spread. Once they operate or do something . . . the inner flesh gets some air. . . It's a known thing, when they open you up." (246:370-374)
Religious Beliefs/ Spirituality	"My friend was probably more worried about it than I was because I'm a strong believer in God and prayer . . . [it] was God's will." (024:79-82)
Breast Cancer and Sexuality	". . . just the idea of having to walk around . . . without a breast. Really, that frightens the daylights out of me and I know someone who had just . . . a lumpectomy . . . She really was messed mentally. She was so worried about her old man, how he would feel because she had been operated on like that and her breasts weren't even anymore . . . She was very, very upset." (246:442-452)
Evaluation of Doctors/Nurses	"She (the doctor) doesn't have that hands-on attitude. She'll talk to you but it's like, she's never taken my pressure. She's never used the stethoscope on me and she just sits and talks and writes. I don't want anybody like that." (246:157-163)

Table 7.2

Continued

Category	Excerpts
	"... I just don't like a man looking at certain parts of my body ... when I went for my ... Pap smear some years back it was a man. I said now why you want to get a job like this for?" (251:266-270)
System Problems	"Well, I'll tell you what I was dissatisfied with. I stayed there all day. From one place to another, and waiting and waiting, and being called and being asked name, telephone number, and address. It was an all day thing. . . . I knew they were professional people, but they didn't treat me that way." (262:67-74)
Financial Issues	"I think that we as black women, it seems that we are not always financially able to get these treatments and what have you, but if there's any way possible for us to get some financial aid or help . . . I think really we should do it. Because our life span is very short as it is." (246:558-569)

*Study ID numbers and text line numbers in parentheses.

By defining the perimeter, they help us understand the center. Because qualitative researchers do not usually assert that their findings are representative or generalizable, this approach is not a problem.

It is difficult to overestimate the importance of being able to think abstractly and conceptually during every stage of qualitative data analysis. When we use concepts in social work, we have a repertoire of familiar ones—resilience, empowerment, and ego strength are a few examples from the practice lexicon. The mental discipline needed to remain open to new ideas and to assign labels that reflect their substantive content does not come easily, but it is the essence of qualitative inquiry.

THE PROS AND CONS OF USING COMPUTER SOFTWARE PROGRAMS

Qualitative data analysis requires a system for coding and retrieval of chunks of text, for organizing codes and themes into files, and for memoing and annotating data-analysis decisions. The old-fashioned way of doing this is rather straightforward: One makes at least two "hard" copies of the data, stores one set of copies for backup, and cuts and pastes from the other set. These excerpts are filed into folders labeled by topic or category. When a particular category (folder) begins to grow, it is further subdivided into subcategories (and separate folders). This is usually done on the dining room table or any flat surface large enough to accommodate the growing volume of data.

With the advent of personal computers, code-and-retrieval of data became possible using word-processing software. Thus, interviews and fieldnotes can be transcribed and edited, memos can be logged, and portions of text can be blocked out, "cut and pasted," and transported into separate data files with relative ease. For many qualitative researchers, word-processing programs are sufficient for the task.

Computer programs developed specifically for qualitative data analysis have proliferated since the 1980s. Like all personal computer software, these programs are constantly being refined and upgraded. Indeed, the pace of change is so rapid that it is unwise to offer more than an overview of what these programs do and their basic features. If you decide to use specialized software, it is best to obtain updated information directly from the software distributors or from authors who specialize in this area such as Miles and Weitzman (1994), Tesch (1991), and Richards and Richards (1994). Names and addresses of distributors (along with references for additional reading) are provided in Appendix A.

Your decision about whether to use computer software programs for data analysis should rest largely on your computer abilities and your needs as a qualitative researcher. If you feel relatively at ease using computers and expect to be doing qualitative research for some time in the future, the investment of time and expense in purchasing and using a specialized program may be well worthwhile.

If you decide to go in this direction, you have many choices in qualitative data-analysis programs. First, be advised that some exclusively use DOS and others just use MacIntosh-based operating systems. If you are a DOS person, this is probably not the time to convert to the Mac way of life and vice versa.

The basic distinction is between qualitative data programs that "code-and-retrieve" and those designed to build theory. Code-and-retrieve programs divide the text into coded chunks, attach codes to the chunks, and search and display these coded chunks (Miles & Weitzman, 1994). Some allow you to list frequencies of codes, the sources of the codes (locations in the text), and hierarchical connections between codes (e.g., "diet" and "exercise" can be connected to the higher order code "self care".) Examples of these programs include The Ethnograph, HyperQual, Hyper-RESEARCH, QUALPRO, and NUD•IST (see Appendix A).

Theory-building programs have code-and-retrieve capabilities, but have the additional capacity to organize codes hierarchically to develop conceptual frameworks that become theoretical propositions for testing. Thus, the researcher can test hypotheses about code co-occurrences in the text, attach memos to text segments, and search for linkages between codes. Perhaps not surprisingly, the logic underlying these programs requires some time to learn and understand.

The greater efficiency afforded by computer software includes the ability to sort, create files, reformat files as they change, and print out reconstituted files with ease. At the same time, the "front-end" process of inputting data and learning how to use the program can be time consuming and frustrating even for those with computer skills. (Some of my more computer-savvy colleagues feel that mastering the software's quirks takes more time than is saved later on.)

Computers have one definite drawback—they do not allow the "simultaneous visual access to materials that makes ideas happen" (Agar, 1991, p. 193). In other words, there is no substitute for spreading out data on the dining room table to look for patterns. Computer screens cannot give us such a panoramic view. No matter how helpful computers are, they can never do the thinking for us.

MOVING FROM CODES TO THEMES

After we abstract codes from the raw data, we look for relations between codes or categories to begin formulating *themes*. Themes arc across wide swaths of the data and capture patterns of human experience. They may jump out at you early on or they may emerge subtly over time. To keep track, you may wish to use color coding or some other system to identify the various categories that fit into a theme.

Respondents may themselves offer *emic* themes. For example, an elderly man might refer to different crises in his life and repeat a mantra about himself: "I am a survivor" or "my life has been a failure." Emic themes have obvious salience because they reflect the respondent's point of view.

Qualitative researchers who choose *narrative analysis* (Mishler, 1986; Riessman, 1993) are likely to bring emic themes to the foreground of the qualitative report, presenting lengthy narratives (rather than coded segments of the data) to respect the integrity of the respondents' story. This analytic decision must be made early on, because it focuses on each respondent's story as an integral whole rather than as,the basis for extraction of various codes that cut across the data.

The movement from codes to themes involves ever higher levels of abstraction and conceptualization. For example, if you are interviewing teenagers in an inner-city neighborhood about their experiences with violence, you might first code different types of violence, for example, sexual abuse and harassment, physical abuse, and verbal threats. You might also wish to distinguish between witnessing violent acts and experiencing them firsthand. Each of these classifications of violence can be illustrated by selected excerpts from the transcripts, by vignettes of experiences of single respondents, or by a lengthier case study of a single adolescent's life.

As linkages between codes are discovered, themes begin to take shape across the sample of respondents. From our hypothetical study of violence, the following themes might emerge: coping with an abusive parent, peer pressures to commit violent acts, the trauma of witnessing violence, gender differences in sexual victimization, and so forth.

Regardless of how the analysis unfolds, the highest levels of abstraction involve linking the study back into the extant knowledge base—both theoretical and empirical. Are the findings consistent with the literature? Do they expand on what we already know or do they debunk received wisdom about the topic?

Although an emic perspective is an invaluable part of qualitative research, the ultimate contribution of a qualitative study depends on the probity and intellectual clarity of the etic analysis—reflections on the meaning and interpretation of the study's findings from the researcher's perspective.

USING NUMBERS IN
QUALITATIVE DATA ANALYSIS

Although some of the more ardent advocates of qualitative research might recoil in horror, there are often good reasons to use numbers in analyzing and presenting qualitative data. A study can even cease being qualitative during data analysis and rely almost exclusively on statistical analyses of quantitative findings.

We may record, for example, the number of interviews conducted, the number of months in the field, and the duration range of interviews (e.g., 1 to 5 hours). We also may use numbers to portray the demographic characteristics of the sample or the percent fitting into a particular typology that we created. The judicious use of numbers need not detract from the narrative premise of most qualitative reports (a topic to be addressed in more depth in Chapter 9).

NEGATIVE CASE ANALYSIS
AND THE QUESTION OF CAUSATION

In qualitative data analysis, the search for *negative cases* corresponds to the quantitative researcher's reliance on a null hypothesis. In both instances, we test our theories by searching for falsifying evidence to refute them. In a sense, we become our own devil's advocate. This follows the logic of philosopher Karl Popper that hypotheses are not truly verified, but only supported in the absence of refuting evidence. Even if we see a million white swans, we can never fully conclude that all swans are white—the sight of only one black swan will falsify this thesis (Guba & Lincoln, 1994). As stated by Albert Einstein, "no amount of evidence can prove me right, and *any* amount of evidence can prove me wrong" (quoted in Miles & Huberman, 1994, p. 242).

In qualitative research, negative case analysis is used in the quest for verification. Let us say that you are interviewing depressed women and detect a pattern of childhood sexual abuse in many of their life stories. This leads you to theorize that childhood abuse is a cause of depression in adulthood. At this point, you are obligated to return to the data to search for negative cases—depressed women who did *not* experience childhood sexual abuse. Finding disconfirming cases need not lead you to completely discard your theory. After all, moderating influences such as strong social support systems may mediate the traumatic effects of the abuse. But it would be a gross violation of research integrity to knowingly suppress negative cases.

The trial-and-error nature of developing and testing theories via negative case analysis fits well with the iterative nature of qualitative inquiry. In our Mammogram Study, the fact that several women mentioned beliefs about "air exposure" as a cause of cancer metastasis led me to hypothesize that these beliefs cause women to delay follow-up treatment after an abnormal mammogram, that is, they delay because they fear that surgery would expose the breast tissue to air and make the cancer spread. The air theory made sense, but it was not borne out by negative case analysis. Indeed, the air theory adherents were no more likely to delay than their nonbelieving counterparts.

It is important to distinguish between *disconfirming* evidence (cases that refute an emerging theory) and *discrepant* evidence (cases that refine an emerging theory) (Goetz & LeCompte, 1984). In the first instance, the exceptional case refutes the rule (e.g., the black swan). In the second instance, it proves the rule but also refines and expands it.

Let us say that you are studying why busy adults volunteer at a soup kitchen and you find that several say that they volunteer as a way of socializing with diverse groups of people. Then your theory about non-altruistic motivation is thrown into question when some volunteers reveal that they lead full social lives. For them, volunteering is a way to "give back" some of their good fortune. Further scrutiny of the interview data reveals that some of the volunteers are college students getting course credit for community service. Although some are enthusiastic, many are grudgingly filling a course requirement. At this point, the negative cases force us to decide whether to refine our theory or discard it altogether.

The line between disconfirming and discrepant cases is blurry at times (Ely et al., 1991). Theories may become so refined and spread so thin that their explanatory value begins to sag under the weight of the evidence. Or you may be so taken with negative case analysis that you disconfirm every theme and achieve a state of analytic paralysis. Somewhere there is a happy medium—a heady mixture of enthusiasm tempered by skepticism. In the meantime, it is probably better to err on the side of caution than to throw it to the wind.

Where does this leave qualitative researchers when questions of causation arise? There is surely no more noble undertaking than generating theories that explain the human experience *and* survive tests of empirical verification. This is also a humbling undertaking, as there are almost always alternative explanations that challenge even the most rigorously designed studies.

Qualitative researchers run the gamut of opinions about causation as a viable goal ranging from relative enthusiasm (Huberman & Miles, 1994) to serious doubt (Lofland & Lofland, 1995). On the sidelines, the antipositivist skeptics question whether the search for causation is even plausible, given the postmodern premise that facts are "fictitious" (Lofland & Lofland, 1995).

As with so many contested issues in qualitative research, one's position here depends in large part on one's epistemological stance. My own inclination is to be cautious and not make promises qualitative research cannot (and probably should not) try to keep. Explanatory theories can be generated from, and tested by, qualitative data. But qualitative study designs do not afford much confidence when it comes to conclusions about causation. I prefer to leave the difficult struggle to determine causation to quantitative researchers.

This need for restraint need not be seen as a damaging limitation of qualitative research. There are countless qualitative studies waiting to be done that can offer rich description and point the way to new avenues for learning.

SUMMARY AND CONCLUSION

A balance of creativity and caution is the hallmark of qualitative data analysis. This chapter introduced the rudiments of data analysis, offering guidelines for organizing the data, developing codes and themes from the data, and testing their validity with negative case analysis.

However, neither this nor any other text can substitute for what can be learned by simply doing—plunging into those transcripts, fieldnotes, and documents in the search for meaning. As with any form of data analysis, quantitative or qualitative, hands-on experience counts the most.

CODA: SUGGESTED CLASSROOM EXERCISES IN QUALITATIVE DATA ANALYSIS

Instructors who have transcripts of qualitative interviews can share portions with their students and ask them to code the interviews. Students then meet in groups and discuss their codes and the reasoning behind them.

Another coding exercise is to ask students to focus on a common experience (such as their reason for going to a school of social work.) They break up into groups of two or three and discuss the topic, focusing on developing a typology. Each group presents its typology to the class for further discussion.

Chapter 8

RIGOR AND RELEVANCE IN QUALITATIVE RESEARCH

One of the most vexing questions surrounding qualitative research involves definitions of *rigor*. Rigor refers to the degree to which a qualitative study's findings are authentic and its interpretations credible (Lincoln & Guba, 1985). To some, problems with rigor are the Achilles heel of qualitative research. Miles and Huberman (1994) wrote about this dilemma: "We have the unappealing double bind whereby qualitative studies can't be verified because researchers don't report on their methodology, and they don't report on their methodology because there are no established canons or conventions for doing so" (p. 244).

Many qualitative researchers take issue with this stance. Janesick (1994), for example, decried "methodolatry"—the slavish attention to method that preoccupies research. Whereas some qualitative researchers argue in favor of separate (nonquantitative) standards for rigor, others question whether such standards are even needed or possible given the "many realities" that qualitative researchers explore. Echoing the concerns of Janesick and others, some social work practitioners have complained that *relevance* has too often been sacrificed on the altar of methodological *rigor* in research (Meyer, 1990).

This sort of "either-or" thinking too often dominates all sides of the epistemological debate. Rigor is essential to all forms of empirical research, whether quantitative or qualitative. It is difficult to see how a nonrigorous study can have relevance. Quantitative studies need not sacrifice relevance and (more important for our task at hand) qualitative studies need not dismiss the need for rigor. We can even have "rigor without rigor mortis" (Gambrill, 1995, p. 43).

In this chapter, I will briefly review the epistemological debate about rigor in qualitative research, discuss some of the threats to credibility of qualitative research, and end with recommendations for strategies to improve rigor and relevance in qualitative research.

THE DEBATE OVER CRITERIA
FOR EVALUATING QUALITATIVE RESEARCH

Taking their cue from Hammersley (1992), Denzin and Lincoln (1994) described a few basic positions arrayed across a continuum of accommodation to (or rejection of) the standards for rigor of quantitative research. I offer these with a good deal of trepidation because use of labels obscures the blurriness of categories and can easily verge into name calling. Such is the volatile nature of epistemological debates.

The more accommodationist of the positions, labeled *positivist*, holds that one set of criteria (that of the scientific method) is sufficient for both quantitative and qualitative research. Few qualitative researchers adhere to this point of view and it seems to exist only in the abstract (or in the minds of some diehard quantitative researchers).

The *postpositivist* position argues for a separate but parallel set of criteria exclusive to qualitative research. There is no consensus on what these criteria should be, although there is general agreement that qualitative studies should emulate the scientific method in striving for empirical groundedness, generalizability, and minimization of bias (Hammersley, 1992). Both the positivist and postpositivist positions emerge from a paradigm that posits an external reality that can be observed and described.

The *constructivists* offer alternative ways of thinking about rigor in research. For some, alternative terms for reliability and validity are offered such as *trustworthiness* (Lincoln & Guba, 1985) and *reflexive accounting* (Altheide & Johnson, 1994). Others turn to the humanities for standards of quality control (Altheide & Johnson, 1994; McCracken, 1988). McCracken (1988), for example, argued that the fields of history, philosophy, and literature offer standards for interpretation and scholarship that can be applied to qualitative studies. The terminology of evaluative criteria in the humanities—elegance, consistency and coherence—may appear vague and imprecise to positivist ears, but constructivists counter that fine scholarship has emerged from the humanistic tradition without the assistance of quantitative methods (McCracken, 1988).

The constructivist position is further along the continuum away from positivism. To constructivists, knowledge is not discovered but is created, a product of the perspective of the observer. Thus, "social realism" is seen as a mistaken belief in a single reality when there are multiple realities created by each observer in the field.

Still further along the continuum are those who reject the premise of evaluative criteria altogether. A number of qualitative researchers have argued that parochial concerns about reliability and validity are irrelevant in qualitative research (Ellis & Flaherty, 1992; Wolcott, 1994). Many feminist researchers, critical theorists, and postmodernists believe that the search for criteria privileges some approaches over others and that the multiplicity of interpretive "truths" precludes any search for standards applicable across the board. Objectivity is an ephemera embraced only by the reductionist number-crunchers of the scientific realm.

Competing paradigms notwithstanding, it is difficult to dispute the argument that research is deeply influenced by where the researcher is situated epistemologically and by the social and political context surrounding the research enterprise (Denzin, 1994). But it is quite another step to conclude that evaluative criteria are unnecessary. If one rejects all criteria as hegemonic, the door is open to intellectual guruism where judgments of scholarly work are left to the whims of a self-anointed academic elite.

Although not an easy task, the pursuit of rigor is, I believe, necessary to legitimize qualitative research as a viable means of producing knowledge and to make it accessible to researchers in a variety of settings inside or outside of academia. In social work research, where findings are ultimately valued for their contributions to policy and practice, rigorous research is also an ethical responsibility (Myers & Thyer, 1997).

Issues in Defining Rigor in Qualitative Research

Just as the relevance versus rigor argument is a false dichotomy, it is misleading to posit that quantitative research is mechanistic and heartless and qualitative studies are warm and caring (Denzin, 1994). Many famous scientists made their breakthrough discoveries by serendipity rather than by plodding through controlled trials in a laboratory (Kirk & Miller, 1986). Scientists may even feel passionate about their work.

Whereas scientific methods discourage (or forbid) a close relationship between experimenter and participant, the results of scientific investigations have been used to bring about humane policy changes—the ultimate form of caring. Striving for *objectivity* need not lead to *objectifying* one's research participants to the point of exploitation. By the same token, the qualitative researcher's caring ethos may, if taken too far, rob the qualitative study of needed rigor and thus render its findings suspect.

The pursuit of rigor in qualitative research requires that we reexamine and even reject some of the canons of the positivist paradigm. For example, *replication* of findings is a hallmark of the scientific method and the basis for inferential statistics where one seeks to guard against chance as an explanation for the findings. Even the most impeccably designed and conducted study humbly concludes with a call for replication.

For qualitative researchers, replication is not a goal, nor is it considered feasible as one cannot recreate the original conditions of an "uncontrolled" field study. Because qualitative studies are less concerned with normative data than with the wide range of life experiences, the validation of findings via replication is not an overriding concern.

Anthropologists have been grappling with this issue for some time. The controversy that raged in the 1970s over the validity of Margaret Mead's observations of Samoan society bolstered her critics' assertions that ethnographic observation and interpretation are riddled with subjectivity. Until relatively recently, the act of restudying another anthropologist's field site was considered poaching, an inflammatory breach of etiquette (Agar, 1980). But the trend toward postmodernism in anthropology has led to revisiting field sites as well as published ethnographic works—a form of reflexive critique considered necessary to purge anthropology of its pretensions of scientific Truth. In its postmodern era, the field of anthropology celebrates rather than condemns multiple perspectives (Geertz, 1983; Rabinow & Sullivan, 1979; Rosaldo, 1989). Data quality control—if considered at all—is evaluated by particularistic criteria such as the fieldworker's training, time in the field, and language abilities. In this context, scientific replication is an impossible (and unwelcome) goal.

Other strategies for scientific rigor do not easily apply to qualitative methods, including *random sampling, generalizability,* and *reliable and valid measurement.* As discussed in Chapter 5, *random sampling* conflicts with the qualitative researcher's need to target specific types of informants. Similarly, *generalizability* is not a priority in qualitative studies, where the uniqueness of the human experience is celebrated (Donmoyer, 1990). Finally, the search for *reliable and valid measurement* via quantification of concepts and psychometric testing is incompatible with the emergent nature of conceptual frameworks in qualitative research.

What do we substitute for these? In qualitative research, the key issue is *trustworthiness* (Guba & Lincoln, 1985). A trustworthy study is one that is carried out fairly and ethically and whose findings represent as closely as possible the experiences of the respondents (Steinmetz, 1991). Trustworthiness is not a matter of blind faith, but must be earned by rigorous scholarship.

THREATS TO THE TRUSTWORTHINESS
OF QUALITATIVE STUDIES

There are a number of threats to the credibility and trustworthiness of qualitative research (Lincoln & Guba, 1985) and most fall under three broad headings: *reactivity, researcher biases,* and *respondent biases.*

Reactivity refers to the potentially distorting effects of the qualitative researcher's presence in the field. How are we interfering with the naturalism of the setting—the behaviors, attitudes, and feelings that we seek to understand in situ?

A second source of distortion comes from the *researcher's biases.* The temptation to filter one's observations and interpretations through a lens clouded by preconceptions and opinions can plague even the most meticulously designed and well-intentioned qualitative study. Investigators may deliberately choose informants who appear simpatico with their world view, may ask leading questions during interviews to get the answers they want, or may ignore data that do not support their conclusions.

There are also emotional pitfalls that can contribute to researcher biases. The unwary qualitative researcher may veer too far in either direction— "going native" or becoming too alienated from the respondents and the field situation to continue being an effective researcher. Maintaining an "emotional middle distance" (Weiss,1994) requires self-discipline on the part of the researcher.

Finally, we have the threat that comes from *respondents' biases.* Respondents may withhold information and even lie to protect their privacy or to avoid revealing some unpleasant truths. At the other extreme, they may try to be "helpful" and offer answers that they believe we want to hear. In either case, we are being led astray.

The threats posed by reactivity and by biases emanating from the researcher and the researched afflict virtually all studies of human beings, whether quantitative or qualitative. But the intensity of the research relationship and the pivotal role of the researcher-as-instrument place qualitative studies in "triple jeopardy" when it comes to these threats. Fortunately, there are a number of ways to reduce their impact and enhance the trustworthiness of the qualitative study.

GUIDELINES FOR RIGOR
IN QUALITATIVE RESEARCH

Imagine that you are writing a qualitative research proposal and you must convince a skeptical audience (a doctoral committee or a funding source) that your study will provide findings of value. This presumption of skepticism is not unfounded since qualitative research is still considered exotic in many circles. Even when viewed favorably, qualitative methods are easily misunderstood by faculty and proposal reviewing committees accustomed to quantitative studies.

What should you do? A pragmatic approach would be to incorporate a section into the proposal explaining the rationale for using qualitative methods and defending their value and logic (Marshall & Rossman, 1995; Morse, 1994; Munhall, 1994). Although this may appear an unfair burden (quantitative researchers need not do this), it can nonetheless inspire greater confidence in the methods and in you, the research instrument.

A qualitative study should address a number of questions in defending its soundness (Marshall & Rossman, 1995). How credible are the findings and the criteria for rigor employed by the investigator? Although the exact conditions of the study cannot be replicated, would a similar investigation yield findings roughly congruent with the original study? How replicable are the study's interpretations given the same set of data? Can we be sure that the study's findings are valid representations and not simply concocted by a biased researcher?

From these questions emerge certain assumptions and guidelines for assessing rigor. Some qualitative researchers turn to the *constructivist* approach espoused by Lincoln and Guba (1985) because it provides a set of terms that are analogous (but not identical) to the terminology of quantitative research. Thus, the *internal validity, external validity, reliability,* and *objectivity* of quantitative studies have their analogues in the *credibility, transferability, auditability,* and *confirmability* of qualitative studies (Lincoln & Guba, 1985). Other qualitative researchers do not follow the constructivist approach, but nonetheless take rigor seriously.

The rejection of conventional scientific terminology by most qualitative researchers underscores their independent stance in defining their research aims and procedures. Thus, concerns about internal validity—the ability to rule out alternative causal explanations of an outcome—do not apply to qualitative studies that reject causal thinking. We already saw that external validity (generalizability) may or may not be seen as desirable by qualitative researchers. Similarly, reliability and objectivity may be viewed as unattainable (or irrelevant).

SIX STRATEGIES FOR ENHANCING RIGOR

Thus far, we have seen how many of the canons of scientific methods are a poor fit for qualitative research. In this section, I will discuss a number of strategies for enhancing rigor and trustworthiness in qualitative research. Although not all are relevant or feasible to carry out in every study, they represent an array of techniques consonant with the aims of qualitative research.

As shown in Figure 8.1, I have identified six strategies for enhancing rigor, each addressing one or more of the threats to trustworthiness described earlier. These strategies are not necessarily exhaustive or mutually exclusive, but they represent the most commonly used (and recommended) procedures for quality control in qualitative research.

Prolonged Engagement

The hallmark of qualitative research, a trait that sets it apart as a form of inquiry, is *prolonged engagement* in the field. Arising from the early days of anthropological fieldwork in far-away places, prolonged engagement has come to be a defining characteristic of qualitative studies regardless of where they take place.

As shown in Figure 8.1, prolonged engagement helps to ameliorate the effects of reactivity and respondent bias. For example, the effects of the researcher's presence dissipates considerably when he spends long periods of time in the field and becomes accepted (or at least tolerated).

Prolonged engagement makes withholding information or lying by respondents less likely. As Eliot Liebow (1993) noted in his study of homeless women, "lies do not really hold up well over long periods of time" (p. 321). A trusting relationship between the researcher and her respondents reduces the motivation as well as the opportunity for deception.

THREAT TO TRUSTWORTHINESS

STRATEGY	Reactivity	Researcher Bias	Respondent Bias
Prolonged Engagement	+	-	+
Triangulation	+	+	+
Peer Debriefing/ Support	0	+	0
Member Checking	+	+	+
Negative Case Analysis	0	+	0
Audit Trail	0	+	0

+   Positive effect in reducing threat
-    Negative effect in reducing threat
0   No effect

Figure 8.1. Strategies for Enhancing Rigor and Trustworthiness

Once a respondent has given informed consent to participate in the study, it seems unlikely that he or she would cooperate just to trick the researcher. Lengthy interviews make it hard to maintain an untruthful story for long.

An experienced researcher can often tell when respondents are shading the truth or willfully lying about some event or behavior. Sometimes the truth only comes out by the second or third (or fourth) interview. The teenager who always practices safe sex, the police officer who has never witnessed police brutality, and the military officer who has never had gay men under his command—these are statements whose ultimate truth can only be ascertained in a trusting, engaged relationship.

Some qualitative researchers argue that even false stories are meaningful because they represent the respondent's choice in framing events. At other times, respondents do not fabricate but simply interpret events through their own filters. In our Mammogram Study, one of the women stated that she had not received her (abnormal) mammogram results when we had independent verification that she had been notified. It was only through probing that we found that her understanding of "results" meant actual receipt of the X-ray film! In this instance, the physician had the "results" and told her about them.

It is the researcher's responsibility to decide when truth matters and when it does not. Focusing too literally on truthfulness can blind us to one truism—qualitative data are rife with personal opinions and feelings.

One drawback of prolonged engagement is the risk of researcher bias. Researchers can go too far in either direction—they can "go native" and lose all interpretive distance or experience the "familiarity breeds contempt" problem and become biased against their respondents. Even so, the advantages of prolonged engagement far outweigh the disadvantages (see Figure 8.1).

Triangulation

The term *triangulation,* borrowed from navigational science and land surveying, refers to using two or more sources to achieve a comprehensive picture of a fixed point of reference. Like binocular vision in humans, reliance on multiple sources of information yields clearer and deeper observation. Although rejected by postmodernists who argue that there are no "fixed points" of anything (Denzin & Lincoln, 1994, p. 482), triangulation is widely practiced as a valuable means of enhancing rigor in qualitative research.

Norman Denzin (1978) identified four types of triangulation relevant to a qualitative study:

1. *Theory triangulation*: the use of multiple theories or perspectives to interpret a single set of data
2. *Methodological triangulation*: the use of multiple methods to study a single topic, for example, combining quantitative and qualitative methods in a single study
3. *Observer triangulation*: the use of more than one observer in a single study to achieve intersubjective agreement
4. *Data triangulation*: the use of more than one data source (interviews, archival materials, observational data, etc.)

To these four types, Valerie Janesick (1994) added a fifth: *interdisciplinary triangulation*. This involves the use of more than one discipline in a single study. A social work researcher, for example, might collaborate with a psychologist, sociologist, anthropologist, or historian.

How does one *triangulate by theory*? Data from a study of battered women could be analyzed using Marxist theory, feminist theory, and psychoanalytic theory. This type of triangulation is likely to yield diverse findings that can broaden our perspectives on the phenomenon. The goal is not to corroborate study findings, but to analyze them in different ways and through different theoretical lenses.

When theoretical perspectives clash and conflicting stories emerge from the same data, triangulation by theory does not work as intended. On the other hand, it demonstrates the mutability of interpretations and the impact of theory.

Triangulation by method refers to the deployment of different methodologies in the same study. Combining qualitative and quantitative approaches is the most common triangulation-by-method strategy—we will discuss this in more detail in Chapter 10. We could also accomplish methodological triangulation by using the methods of differing disciplines. In our hypothetical study of battered women, we may use historiographic methods for analyzing archival data and grounded theory methods for analyzing the interview data.

During data collection, we may use multiple observers in the field to *triangulate by observation*. For example, in their ethnographic study of the urban homeless, Snow and Anderson (1991) used multiple observers to enhance the accuracy and reliability of their observations. While analyzing data, we may have multiple coders (*analytic triangulation*) to ensure that the categories and themes that emerge are confirmed by intercoder consensus.

Perhaps the most commonly known type of triangulation is *triangulation by data source*. This refers to the use of different types of data as a means of corroboration. When data from fieldnotes, interviews, and archival materials are convergent and support each other, we can be more confident of our observations and study conclusions.

Qualitative studies typically include fieldnotes and interview data. Archival materials, if they are available and relevant, can be included as well. In our hypothetical study of battered women, for example, we might accumulate data from (a) documents such as shelter records, arrest records from the criminal justice system, and letters and correspondence; (b) interviews with the women, their battering partners, and the shelter staff; and (c) fieldnotes from our observations during many hours spent at the shelter.

It is difficult to overstate the value of triangulation for enhancing the rigor of a qualitative study. As shown in Figure 8.1, triangulation helps to counter all of the threats to trustworthiness. At the same time, we should not be dismayed by inconsistencies and even contradictions when they occur (Mathison, 1988). If and when conflicts emerge between two data sources, we are faced with a decision about which version to rely on. Or we might view these discrepancies as an opportunity for new insights.

On some occasions, triangulation is not what we are after. An assumption of a fixed point of reference—a single verifiable version of something—may not be useful. Riessman (1990), in her study of divorcing partners, found that men and women held very different perspectives about their marital problems and this became a prime focus of her study. The discrepant and even conflicting stories told by spouses about their marital problems became a jumping-off point for an insightful discussion of the different ways that men and women make sense of divorce.

This example illustrates why we should not overreact to inconsistencies and contradictions from triangulated data. Just as *negative case analysis* may reveal cases that disconfirm our interpretations, disagreement among data sources may open our eyes to different perspectives.

Peer Debriefing and Support

Peer support groups have been called a "life line" for qualitative researchers (Steinmetz, 1991). Peer support group participants gather to get and give feedback, offer fresh ideas, and simply recharge their batteries. Because so much depends on the qualitative researcher, wear and tear on the "instrument" can take a toll. Attending a peer support group meeting gives the researcher a chance to share the emotional ups and downs of fieldwork and data analysis.

But the role of these groups in qualitative research is not simply socioemotional. They are also a mechanism for debriefing and guarding against bias, for keeping the researcher "honest" throughout the study (Lincoln & Guba, 1985). To this end, they contribute to the rigor of a qualitative study (see Figure 8.1).

Qualitative researchers can transgress boundaries without conscious intent. They may become too enmeshed in their respondents' lives. During data analysis, they may embark on a tangent of reasoning born of too many hours spent alone with the data. These problems, among others, can be identified and ameliorated by peer group feedback.

Qualitative researchers use peer groups in a number of ways. They may present ideas or hunches to the group for feedback. They may read portions of their coding memos along with relevant chunks of data to see if the codes make sense. Or they may read passages from their fieldnotes and journals to get reactions from others about their observations and their ability to be self-reflexive. There are rarely any set rules as long as confidentiality is maintained and the focus stays on constructive criticism.

Peer support groups work best when they meet on a regular schedule (monthly or bimonthly) and rotate leadership roles among group members. Their composition can be homogeneous by discipline or they may be multidisciplinary. Homogeneous groups allow members to draw on common interests, communicate in a common language, and reduce time spent negotiating disciplinary boundaries. At the same time, heterogeneous groups—qualitative researchers from social work, nursing, sociology, anthropology, and education—can be invigorating when the diverse backgrounds of participants generate fresh insights. For qualitative researchers who do not have access to a peer support group, acquiring even one peer debriefer with qualitative research expertise can be helpful.

In addition to their rigor-enhancing qualities, peer support groups perform instrumental functions. Groups members give helpful hints like remembering to take extra tape recorder batteries to interviews. They share news of the latest in qualitative data analysis software. They encourage participants to set and meet deadlines in completing the project. They might even offer suggestions on how to negotiate with an unhappy partner feeling neglected by the researcher's time spent in the field. Where else can one go for this kind of help? Come to think of it, quantitative researchers could also benefit from this type of support!

Peer support does have a few risks. Groups can collectively veer off course, either by fostering a sort of "group think" atmosphere of enforced conformity or by becoming hypercritical and intolerant (Garner, 1991). New ideas are very fragile creations and can get crushed even by well-meaning colleagues (Wolcott, 1994). If criticism becomes destructive, "peer support" is an oxymoron. In these instances, the group becomes just as biased as any single researcher and may even worsen the situation. When properly led, however, peer support is an invaluable addition to the qualitative researcher's repertoire of rigor enhancement.

Member Checking

As data collection segues into data analysis, qualitative researchers often seek verification of their codes and interpretations by going back to their respondents. *Member checking* (Lincoln & Guba, 1985) involves returning periodically to the field to ensure that one is on the right track. Because respondents' perspectives are not only honored but valued as authoritative, this can be an important step in guarding against researcher bias. It is also a logical extension of the trusting relationship between the researcher and the respondent.

Member checking is not always easy. Some respondents are busy and do not want to be bothered (even if they gave prior consent to a return visit). Respondents may not understand or approve of our interpretations or they may feel chagrined at being asked to return to painful personal material. An agency director, for example, may have second thoughts about what she has told you about mismanagement by mid-level administrators. Or members of an estranged couple may question your interpretation of their accounts of why the marriage failed.

Conflicting perspectives during member checking compel us to revisit the data and our interpretations. At this point, you may wish to stick to your viewpoint (and explain why you feel you must do so) or you may be convinced to withdraw portions of the data or revise your interpretations. This is a tough call that requires a delicate balancing act between respecting the respondents' wishes and serving the needs of the study. The would-be qualitative researcher should take heart: Nonnegotiable disagreements during member checking are relatively rare. They seldom pose barriers to completion of the study.

For some types of studies, member checking may be impossible due to logistical barriers or gatekeeper issues. For example, you might be conducting in-depth interviews around the country and cannot afford the cost of return visits. Or you have permission from a hospital to interview cancer patients, but with the proviso that they are only burdened by one interview. In these instances, we make do with what we have. When possible to carry out, member checking remains one of the most important ways to lend trustworthiness to a qualitative study.

Negative Case Analysis

Although described in greater detail in Chapter 7, the value of *negative case analysis* for enhancing rigor bears repeating here. Just as the peer group challenges a researcher to explore his or her biases, negative case analysis is a sort of self-imposed "devil's advocate" position assumed during data analysis. It can lend enormous credibility to a study.

Auditing—Leaving a Trail

In our efforts to open the black box of qualitative research methods, we leave an *audit trail* so that our findings may be confirmed by others (Lincoln & Guba, 1985). Leaving an audit trail means adopting a spirit of openness and documenting each step taken in data collection and analysis. The components of an audit trail include the raw data—fieldnotes, interview transcripts, and so forth, along with the journal and memos noting decisions made during data collection, coding, and analysis. Although the audit trail is not intended for exact replication, it does enhance *reproducibility,* that is, another researcher is able to use it to reproduce and verify the findings (Schwandt & Halpern, 1988).

As discomfiting as this may be, imagine for the moment that your study is being audited by the research equivalent of the Internal Revenue Service—a Bureau of Rigor in Research (BRR). If audited, could you defend your report and the decisions you made with actual documentation? Or do you find yourself shrugging helplessly and asking the auditor to have faith in your good intentions?

Although no one wants to see a real BRR put into place (a chilling thought), the underlying process of accountability is not an unrealistic expectation these days, as all empirical studies are increasingly scrutinized for quality control. Ideally, a study is audited by an impartial third party with expertise in qualitative methods. In a sense, auditing is a metastrategy for enhancing rigor because it also documents that the other strategies— prolonged engagement, peer support, member checks, triangulation, and negative case analysis—have been used where appropriate.

In addition to verifying that strategies for rigor were followed, the auditor should pay attention to a few key points listed below (Inui & Frankel, 1991):

- Are the findings grounded in the data?
- Are the codes and themes logical and credible? Are alternative hypotheses given their due? Is negative case analysis employed?
- Are fieldnotes relatively value free? Are reflexive concerns about bias (researcher or respondent) kept separately in a journal and in memos?
- Can decisions about sampling, data collection, and analysis be justified? If changes were made during the course of the study, are they reasonable and defensible?

Social work researcher Sandra Beeman (1995) offered a published account of how she addressed rigor in her study of social support and child neglect among low-income African American mothers. Beeman described how steps in the data analysis were documented in a journal and in memo form to external auditors so that the reasoning behind the codes could be assessed and potential biases uncovered and addressed. By elucidating all stages in the data collection and analysis and all strategies deployed for enhancing rigor, she opened up her study to scrutiny by auditors and enhanced its credibility.

SUMMARY AND CONCLUSION— REVISITING THE DEBATE OVER RIGOR IN QUALITATIVE RESEARCH

By now, the reader may be wondering if any stone has been left unturned in our search for rigor in qualitative research. Admittedly, there are difficulties in carrying out these strategies. Providing logistical support for peer debriefing groups can tax the resources of a school. On the individual level, the time commitment necessary for prolonged engagement requires shifting one's life and finances around to support absences from work and home.

On the positive side, the pursuit of rigor in qualitative research is a decidedly "low tech" enterprise. Consider the demands of quality control in quantitative research—data must be entered and cleaned, psychometric analyses must be conducted on the reliability and validity of the measures, confounding variables must be included in the predictive models, and so forth. By comparison, triangulation, member checks, negative case analysis, and even peer debriefing can be accomplished without as much technical expertise and statistical savvy. Computer software may be used, but it is not necessary.

To be sure, the time needed to pursue rigor is not inconsequential. Miles and Huberman (1994) estimated a 20% increase in time expenditures imposed by the need for documentation. But it is difficult to justify cost savings at the expense of rigor. Without at least some effort put forth, our findings would be clouded by suspicion.

Within the family of qualitative methods, epistemological tendencies often dictate which types of rigor strategies make the most sense. For qualitative researchers interested in phenomenological approaches, peer debriefing and auditing are considered potentially contaminating influences that interfere with the search for deep structures of meaning (Garner, 1991). Instead, verification must depend on the internal coherence of the "lived experience" as told by respondents.

Two other sources of concern regarding the pursuit of rigor revolve around ethical issues and the potentially stifling effects of overspecification (Marshall, 1990). Prolonged engagement, peer debriefing, member checks, and auditing all expose respondents to a loss of privacy (Akeroyd, 1991), and sharing one's fieldnotes, diaries, and interview transcripts increases this risk. We must incorporate ethical concerns into our pursuit of rigor.

Some qualitative researchers have complained that documentation can become overly obsessive and drain the researcher's creative energies (Miles & Huberman, 1994; Noblit, 1988). After all, they argued, isn't qualitative research the one place where intuition, improvisation and logic can coexist? Where prose and elegance of expression are valued? Here again, we must find the comfort zone in balancing rigor and relevance. Just as rigor without relevance produces research that is mechanistic and devoid of meaning, relevance without rigor is a dead end when it comes to knowledge building. When qualitative studies soar too far above the clouds and neglect rigor, they risk the ultimate form of irrelevance—research that is misleading or even harmful in its impact on people's lives.

Chapter 9

TELLING THE STORY
Writing Up the Qualitative Study

Qualitative researchers who have a talent for writing and take pleasure in artful expression are truly blessed. They are also rare. For most of us, writing up a qualitative study takes effort. We try to tell a story that soars creatively yet remains firmly grounded in the data. This is not an easy thing to do. This chapter is intended for the vast majority of professionals who do not possess that ineffable ability to produce masterful works of literary art.

The months of fieldwork and data analysis have set the stage for the lonely task of facing the blank page (or computer screen). Our basic goal is to produce a report that is scholarly, trustworthy, and readable. To ignore any of these prescriptions is problematic. In this chapter, I will argue that violating the latter—producing a poorly written qualitative report—is egregious in its own way. Of course, even elegant writing cannot save a weak study.

Mervyn Susser (1997) drew an interesting distinction between "authoring" and "writing" when discussing the dilemma of authorship in the burgeoning research literature. Many journal articles and books are *authored* (and coauthored), but so few of these authors actually *write*. Writing is not merely reporting or translation, it requires original thinking (or at least an original web of ideas created by the writer) (Susser, 1997).

To illustrate this point, consider how most quantitative reports look. Full of numbers and data, their readability takes second place to the need for precision. The terminology of statistical analyses, embedded within a standardized reporting format, produces a writing style that informs but does not captivate. Compared to qualitative studies, quantitative studies are always authored, but not always written.

There are advantages to this standardization in quantitative reporting. I have found the process of writing quantitative reports, undergoing peer review, and revising for publication to be comparatively straightforward activities, less subject to the whims of editors and peer reviewers than qualitative writing. The task of writing up quantitative research is relatively accessible to persons who are not particularly creative or able to write well.

It is quite a different story for qualitative researchers. If the act of writing up quantitative research is pro forma and somewhat anticlimactic (a well-conducted study can usually survive a poor write-up), it is the climactic event in qualitative research—the study can never transcend poor writing.

The very aspects that make qualitative studies so enjoyable to read are those that demand the utmost from the researcher-as-writer. This is not to say that qualitative reports are simply an exercise in Creative Fiction Writing 101. What sets them apart from fiction is their foundation in empirical data.

As we approach writing up the study, we return to the categories, themes, and minitheories that are the heart of our findings. If the data analysis has been organized and productive, the write-up may require little more than pulling together and presenting the main findings. If procrastination or uncertainty has set in, the write-up will take more effort.

Two rather obvious suggestions can help you prepare for writing. First, read as many good qualitative studies as you can (a partial list of suggestions is provided at the end of this chapter). Second, begin writing as soon as possible.

Reading and absorbing both the form and substance of qualitative studies will expose you to the many strategies available for the write-up and help you to develop your own presentational style. But reading is only the beginning. To employ a sports analogy, if reading is like being a spectator, writing is like being a player (Lofland & Lofland, 1995). For the athlete and the writer, there is no substitute for practice.

It is better to write even when you do not feel like it than to wait for a lightning bolt of inspiration to strike (Wolcott, 1990). Start with a detailed outline and flesh it out as you go. Contrary to popular assumptions, difficulties in writing up qualitative research are not due to "writer's block" but to an "idea block" (Lofland & Lofland, 1995, p. 205). Ideas form the connective tissue of a qualitative report. Without them, it is a shapeless mass devoid of intellectual content.

The self-selection process leading some researchers toward qualitative research tends to favor idea-oriented people. Indeed, the opportunity to be creative is one of the great attractions of qualitative research. The challenge is to keep our ideas firmly grounded empirically.

DECIDING ON AN APPROACH: ALIGNING EPISTEMOLOGY, DATA, AND INTERPRETIVE STYLE

The absence of a standard formula for presenting the findings of a qualitative study is liberating, but it also imposes a good deal of conscious decision making on the part of the researcher. Ideally, the write-up flows logically from a well-aligned epistemological stance and study methodology. But this still leaves a number of questions unanswered.

A number of leading qualitative researchers have discussed their own strategies for writing up qualitative research, including John Van Maanen (1988), Harry Wolcott (1990), Margot Ely et al. (1991), Robert Weiss (1994), Norman Denzin (1994), and Laurel Richardson (1990). In reviewing their works and my own writing experience, I have identified five key decisions facing the qualitative researcher approaching the write-up. These are (a) deciding on the audience for the study, (b) deciding whether the study is diachronic or synchronic, (c) deciding where the study falls on the continuum between emic and etic, (d) deciding how much reflexivity should be included, and (e) deciding on whether and how to use numbers.

Targeting Your Audience

Qualitative reports have the potential to reach broad audiences with their accessible, nontechnical style of writing. Some of our best qualitative studies began in academia, but also appealed to diverse audiences far outside the walls of academe. Eliot Liebow's *Talley's Corner* (1967) is a good example of such a study: His portrayal of the daily lives of African American men in a Washington, D.C. neighborhood in the early 1960s continues to captivate readers with its scholarly yet readable format.

Recently, the trend toward disciplinary and topical specialization led qualitative researchers to target their reports to narrower audiences. Indeed, some qualitative studies are so densely analytic (and jargon ridden) that only a few insiders can understand them. Even the more accessible studies evince a level of intellectual refinement that comes at the cost of popular appeal.

TELLING THE STORY   107

Of course, the aim of the qualitative researcher is not to become a best-selling author (as financially tempting as this may sound). A balance needs to be struck between writing a report that is both readable and intellectually stimulating.

Qualitative reports may be written for any one or all of these purposes: as evaluative reports for an agency or foundation, as doctoral dissertations, as class term papers, or as studies intended for presentation and publication. They often do double duty, for example, a dissertation can also be a program evaluation or a class term paper may also become a conference presentation. For each of these intended purposes, consideration of the audience helps shape the report's final form.

For *academic audiences*—doctoral dissertation committees, journal editors, and conference attendees—the write-up will need to be pitched at a high level of abstraction with solid conceptual and theoretical content. The emphasis in an academic report is on how the study offers new and important insights. Thus, one must be creative and innovative or run the risk of stating the obvious and reinventing the wheel. Remember, too, that academic audiences can be daunting—one must be prepared to defend the study's rigor and interpretations.

Evaluative reports and reports written for *practitioner audiences* are usually written in more pragmatic language (less academic-speak) and are structured more toward concrete suggestions for practice and policy. When a study is commissioned and funded, the sponsoring organization usually wants the researcher to assess problems and recommend solutions. As a target audience, the sponsor may also try to influence how the study is written up.

Whereas it is always a good idea to consult with key stakeholders while writing the final report, the researcher must assume ultimate responsibility for producing a report that is as balanced and accurate as possible. The best defense in these situations is to provide clear evidence of rigor and of strategies employed to control bias. It is also wise to negotiate terms that favor rigor and truthfulness *before* the commissioned study begins so that contractual obligations are honored.

Another type of audience—the *general public*—is one that some researchers scorn and others long for. Researchers in social work and other helping professions have an obligation to disseminate their findings to many audiences, including the general public, especially when those findings have implications for social policies. Even the staid *New England Journal of Medicine* prides itself on holding media-saturated press conferences to announce a newly published study's findings.

In reaching the general public, qualitative studies have the advantage of being "reader friendly." On the other hand, the length of qualitative reports and the need to approach their findings holistically render the task of dissemination difficult, especially for audiences with short attention spans (which includes most policymakers and even a few researchers and practitioners).

The benefits of reaching a wider audience lie in providing general readers with an accessible way to be enlightened by empirical research. The drawbacks come when we feel pressures to abbreviate, dilute, or distort our findings to make them more palatable. Regardless of our intended audience, no qualitative study should cut corners when it comes to scholarship and the integrity of the findings.

I believe that rigorous, well-written qualitative studies can reach both *proximal* and *distal* audiences (Lofland & Lofland, 1995). A doctoral dissertation can satisfy the demands of a doctoral committee (proximal audiences) *and* become a widely read book (distal audience). An evaluative report may be well received by the commissioning organization and appeal to community organizations, professionals, and others interested in the program under scrutiny.

In our Mammogram Study, we hope that the results and write-up will provide new insights into cancer prevention and control for our funding source (the National Cancer Institute) and for professionals in cancer control—our proximal audiences. Although I entertain occasional fantasies of national television and radio coverage of our study's findings, this is not our ultimate goal. But we do have a distal audience—all persons who care about breast cancer and its detection and treatment.

Diachronic Versus Synchronic Reports

As discussed in Chapter 7, a fundamental decision in qualitative research centers on the element of time. All qualitative studies are longitudinal in a sense—prolonged engagement demands no less. But how the writer chooses to deal with the element of time depends on the study goals. This decision, in turn, structures the presentation of the findings (Weiss, 1994).

A *diachronic* report, for example, tells a story through time. It is often focused on how people respond to important life events or crises and is often structured around stages of adjustment. You may be studying how parents adjust to the birth of a child with severe defects, how an elderly gay man lives with AIDS, or how the staff at a Planned Parenthood clinic cope with violent protests by an antiabortion group. Whether you track the event before it occurs, as it is ongoing, or only in its aftermath, the thrust of the report is oriented toward change over time.

Diachronic reports also chronicle "normal" developmental changes in people's lives—the birth of a baby, entering college, or retiring from the workforce. They may capture the dense emotionality of the lives of "average" people or they may document the life stories of extraordinary persons whose lives exemplify important social or historical trends. Regardless of their substantive content, diachronic reports have a structure that is sequential and time based.

In contrast to diachronic reports, *synchronic* reports freeze time, collapsing months or years of fieldwork into a report structured around static (but rich) description. In the social sciences, the types of synchronic studies that prevailed before the 1960s were *structural-functionalist* in approach. The structural-functionalist study described how a system worked, whether it was an individual, a family, a village, or small town. By the 1960s, structural-functionalism came under attack by critics who argued that the approach celebrated the status quo and neglected internal dysfunction as well as external forces of oppression.

Of course, synchronic reports of qualitative research need not be structural-functionalist in the sense of supporting the status quo. The researcher may opt for an activist approach, framing the findings in terms of advocacy for change.

To illustrate how synchronic reports can emphasize rich description or advocacy, let us say that you are studying women in prison. If your concern is with the texture of their lives, you may focus on the problems they face (the loss of their children, getting along with other inmates, resisting sexual advances by prison guards) as well as their resilience (enrolling in prison education programs, divorcing an abusive spouse). This type of synchronic report draws the reader into their lives; it is informative without having an overt agenda.

On the other hand, you may be concerned with the plight of imprisoned women, many of whom are serving time for minor drug offenses after a lifetime of physical and sexual abuse. The report may document how these emotionally scarred women became involved with drug use, prostitution, and abusive partners, pointing to the need for reform in the criminal justice system to better address their needs.

Of course, the distinction between richly descriptive and action-oriented synchronic reports is often blurry. The difference is largely one of emphasis and intent. Similarly, the distinction between synchronic and diachronic is not always clear-cut. In their study of hospital-based physicians and social workers, Mizrahi and Abramson (1994) developed a tripartite typology to explain how these professionals approached collaboration with one another—traditional, transitional, and transformational. This typology represented a continuum of accommodation (or resistance) to the social worker's autonomy in her collaborative role with the physician.

Taken at face value, this typology is an informative, but static, description of the working relationships of physicians and social workers. But Mizrahi and Abramson took a step toward diachronic reporting by pointing out the dynamic nature of these collaborative styles, how physicians and social workers can adopt differing approaches over time in response to new exigencies. This makes sense, particularly given the rapid pace of change in hospital staffing and management under managed care.

Robert Weiss (1994) suggested that diachronic reports have the advantage of a built-in story line that synchronic reports do not share. This is true as far as it goes, but both diachronic and synchronic reports run the risk of *underconceptualization.* This rather unwieldy term describes a study that is more impressionistic than scholarly. It may be interesting to read but the absence of a conceptual framework renders it unconnected to the world of ideas.

The Emic-Etic Continuum

The emic versus etic dichotomy is a useful heuristic device for reintroducing standpoint strategy—discussed earlier in Chapter 7. The standpoint adopted by writers of qualitative studies until the 1970s was largely etic. Characterized as "Realist Tales" by Van Maanen (1988), these studies were written in the third person with little or no recognition of the researcher's role in producing the findings. The author's authority was taken for granted, the story told as received truth by an unseen (and unsung) observer. To use first-person pronouns in the text was an unthinkable breach of etiquette, unscientific and self-indulgent. Ironically, writers of Realist Tales spent countless hours regaling colleagues and friends with stories of their experiences in the field—experiences that undoubtedly played a role in shaping the study but were edited out of the final report (Van Maanen, 1988).

The changes in interpretive writing styles that accompanied the rise of constructivism and postmodernism in the 1970s directly challenged the etic approach. Academic and general audiences came to accept (and even value) reports that included first-person narratives by respondents and by researchers.

According to its more vociferous critics, the etic approach in qualitative research is arid and context stripping—an accusation that would make any self-respecting qualitative researcher cringe. To these critics, the human emotions stirred by fieldwork are squeezed out of the etic report in favor of a "didactic deadpan style" (Van Maanen, 1988, p. 36). Thus, a "Doctrine of Immaculate Perception" (Van Maanen, 1988, p. 73) obscures the vividness and ambiguity that define qualitative research.

I suspect that some of this criticism is a bit overwrought, a sincere but misguided attempt to hasten the postmodern millenium with its paradigm shift away from logical positivism. Despite its derogation, the etic approach in some form remains an essential element of most qualitative reports.

However, just as a purely etic approach is to be avoided, one can go too far with emicism. Eliminating the researcher's standpoint from the write-up reduces her to the role of an unthinking conduit and undermines the scholarly impact of the report. Of course, it could be argued that there is no such thing as a purely emic study—the mere act of sorting and presenting the data imposes an editorial standpoint. But any study that purports to "tell the respondent's story" with little or no authorial interpretation runs the risk of overdoing emicism.

I believe the ideal compromise is to blend the two approaches, juxtaposing emic accounts with codes, analysis, and intrepretation by the author. Suggestions for how to do this will follow later in this chapter.

Reflexivity—How Much Is Too Much?

It is abundantly clear by now that the researcher is a key actor in the qualitative study and should be acknowledged as such in the report. What remains open to question is how prominently that role should be featured. If taken too far, *reflexivity* produces unauthorized autobiography and tedious self-absorption. Yet, so much of one's experience in the field—failures as well as successes—is pertinent to the findings and the ultimate credibility of the study.

Maintaining reflexivity during data collection and analysis is an ongoing task. As discussed in the previous chapter, member checks, peer groups, and audits enhance reflexivity by encouraging self-awareness and self-correction. But the decision about how reflexive we should be in the final report—how much of our personal selves and experiences we include—is not an easy one to make. Moreover, this decision is closely linked to where the study falls on the etic-emic continuum.

Figure 9.1 shows a 2 × 2 typology of qualitative reports based on the dichotomies of emic-etic and reflexive-nonreflexive styles of reporting. The first type, that of etic nonreflexive writing, is the Traditional Approach. Realist Tales (Van Maanen, 1988) constitute an enormously influential archive of qualitative research conducted during the 20th Century.

The second type of report, emic but nonreflexive, emerged after World War II. Influenced by the rise of ethnomethodology in anthropology, postwar emic research was designed to elicit the respondent's world view without imposing Eurocentric systems of classification and interpretation. If any categories were reported, they were indigenous, not investigator initiated. More recent phenomenological approaches follow in this tradition, seeking to portray the "lived experience" without interpretive filters (Denzin & Lincoln, 1994; Holstein & Gubrium, 1994).

Intended to remedy the misguided "scientific" detachment of early ethnography, emicism eschewed grand theories of culture and society and instead sought to convey the richness and structure of native taxonomies and experience. However, the shift of standpoint from the objective truths of Immaculate Perception (Van Maanen, 1988) to the lived experience of the Other does not necessarily entail reflexivity on the part of the researcher. Thus, the Ethnomethodological Approach to qualitative reports is emic but not reflexive.

A third type of qualitative study—the Bifurcated Approach—represents an attempt at compromise. Typically, the main body of the report is etic, comprising the "official report" of the study's findings. Reflexive discussions of what happened behind the scenes—the author's field experiences and their impact on the study—are reserved for another part of the report.

Many qualitative writers present an "official study" and reserve reflexivity discussions for an appendix. These appendices reveal the decisions made during data collection and analysis, the epistemological stance (or stances) assumed by the author during the study, and the trials and tribulations of carrying out the study. Aside from providing fascinating first-person accounts of life in the field, these frank discussions inspire confidence that the author is aware of the pitfalls of researcher bias and has tried to grapple with them.

When the researcher's experiences take center stage in the qualitative report, a Confessional Approach is used (Van Maanen, 1988). As shown in Figure 9.1, both etic-style objectivity and nonreflexivity are dropped in this approach. Even emicism is redefined, focusing more on the author's perspectives rather than those of the respondent.

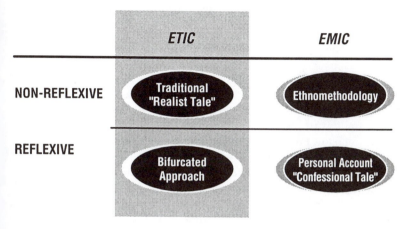

Figure 9.1. A Typology of Qualitative Reports

Some qualitative researchers view the Confessional Tale as a welcome opportunity to discard the staid expository style of academic writing (Richardson, 1994). When the spotlight shifts to the researcher, there is no need to strive for truthfulness or empirical verifiability. Feminist and postmodern researchers have been on the forefront in promoting this approach. Whereas their objections to etic research are well known, they also argue that ethnomethodological approaches are misguided in assuming the existence of a "clear window into the inner lives of individuals" (Denzin & Lincoln, 1994, p. 12). As all observations are filtered through the lens of the observer's gender, race, age, and social class, qualitative reports cannot present objective Truth whether etically or emically derived.

Although rarely acceptable as the sole product of a qualitative study, Confessional Tales can perform a useful function as cautionary tales. By describing how the best-laid plans can go wrong in the field, they imply that norms exist. Perhaps inadvertently, confessional accounts acknowledge the need for rigor even as they expose its difficulties (Van Maanen, 1988).

When a qualitative study veers off course into unforeseen directions, the researcher may feel it more instructive to tell a confessional tale than a misbegotten realist tale. A good example of this from social work research is Cheryl Hyde's (1994) account of her study of feminist organizations, a zig-zag personal journey with unanticipated consequences. As she traveled around the country interviewing leaders of feminist organizations, Hyde was forced to examine her own reactions (including dislike for some feminist leaders) and to continually change her study to meet new exigencies.

Confessional tales are fun to read—who doesn't enjoy hearing about the trials and tribulations of others? They also have tremendous popularity among critics of positivism who delight in the way such tales expose the human frailties of researchers. But even their proponents are concerned that the trend toward confessionalism has gone too far, giving rise to "more reflexive than thou" positions (Marcus, 1994, p. 568) where researchers accuse one another of insufficient reflexivity and compete to produce the most humble confessions of mea culpa.

Imagine a scenario where our respondents find out that our study is not about them at all. We learned a lot from them, but the real story is about *us*! If confessionalism becomes a modus operandi, we misuse and are likely to mislead our respondents. I can think of few respondents who would (or should) give informed consent to such a solipsistic endeavor!

Van Maanen (1988) sensibly stated that Confessional Tales do not replace Realist Tales, but function best as supplementary reading. Personal reflections by the researcher-as-instrument are difficult to justify except as vehicles for improvement of the methodology.

Using Numbers in the Report

Perhaps less weighty is the decision about whether to use numbers in writing up the final report. Numerical findings such as frequencies and percents can enhance the qualitative report. Similarly, when presenting a code or category, you may want to report the number of times it appeared or the number of respondents who reported it.

In a study of care-giving daughters and their elderly mothers, Walker and Allen (1991) identified three relationship types (intrinsic, ambivalent, and conflicted) and the percent of mother-daughter pairs for each type (45%, 34%, and 21%, respectively). Providing indices of the proportion fitting into each of the three categories helps the reader to understand how these types were distributed among the 29 mother-daughter pairs who were studied.

A few caveats pertain to using numbers in qualitative reports. First given the nonrepresentativeness and small sample sizes in qualitative studies, we should treat numerical findings gingerly and avoid giving a false impression of precision where none exists. Small numbers can also lead to unusual chance findings. Let us say that you are studying 15 Korean American immigrant women and 9 of them report being physically abused by their husbands. Should you report this as a numerical finding? By doing so, will your report unwittingly convey the message that 60% of Korean American immigrant women are abused? Concerns about the misuse or misunderstanding of qualitative findings should not prevent us from reporting this information, but we should responsibly explain the dangers of generalizing from such a small sample.

Numbers are most useful when presenting findings that are central to a study. For example, "10 agency directors (40% of those who participated in the study) lost their jobs during the course of the study." In the example of the study of mother-daughter pairs by Walker & Allen (1991) mentioned previously, it made sense to introduce the three types and then offer the percent of pairs fitting into each type.

There are also occasions when using *most* or *some* to convey the extent of something is sufficient (Weiss 1994). Thus, "most of the women in the study expressed satisfaction with their medical care" sounds better than "80% were satisfied with their medical care" when "80%" refers to 8 out of 10 women.

Sometimes even one incident is worth reporting. Let us say that you are studying how the mentally disabled cope with cutbacks in SSI (Supplementary Security Income). Fearing eviction, one of your respondents becomes despondent and commits suicide. This tragic event illustrates in stark terms the human consequences of policy changes. To omit it from the report because it is an atypical response seems to be missing out on what qualitative research does best. Our never-ending search for patterns in human experience should not prevent us from reporting singular cases or incidents that illuminate the outer boundaries of human experience.

Another caveat when reporting numbers or counts of things is this: Remember that many important findings from qualitative studies were *not routinely elicited.* Unlike in standardized surveys, valuable information in qualitative research is often volunteered, but not solicited routinely. As such, any count of the number of respondents who give certain information probably represents an undercount of the phenomenon in question.

For example, in a preliminary analysis of qualitative data from the Mammogram Study, 8 out of 28 women (28%) mentioned the "air theory" as a possible cause of the spread of breast cancer (Padgett, Yedidia, Kerner, & Mandelblatt, 1996). Although this may seem a small proportion, we can be reasonably certain that more of the women would have expressed a belief in the air theory if we had asked them about it. (Indeed, after our interviewers began to probe further when asking respondents about how cancer spreads, the proportion of women who mentioned the air theory rose dramatically in subsequent interviews.)

ORGANIZING THE REPORT— FOUR KEY COMPONENTS

As mentioned previously, the creative latitude a qualitative researcher is allowed in writing the final report is substantial, depending in part on the intended audience. Although no consensual guidelines exist, the majority of qualitative reports contain the following key components (Munhall, 1994):

1. *The goals and background of the study.* Here, the author describes the phenomenon of interest, provides a rationale for the study, and offers a literature review placing the study within a theoretical and historical context.

2. *The method of inquiry: general and applied.* This section tends to be placed in the body of doctoral dissertations and consigned to an appendix in books that are marketable. The first part introduces the reader to qualitative research in general and to the method of inquiry (grounded theory, phenomenology, feminist theory, etc.). Here, we educate the reader about qualitative research and provide a rationale for using qualitative methods. The second part of the method section gives a detailed description of how the study's goals were accomplished. Here, the author describes the hows, whens, and whys of the study: site and sample selection, entering the field and establishing rapport, the setting(s) of the study, data collection procedures, storing and sorting of data, data analyses and coding decisions, ethical concerns and human subjects considerations, and strategies deployed for ensuring rigor. The author should be candid about the limitations of the study's methodology and his or her role as the instrument of data collection and analysis.

3. *Findings.* This section is the heart of the matter. All of your best efforts at insight and creativity are framed conceptually and placed on the table for the reader to absorb. There are many choices available to the writer; the only requirement is that the findings are readable and rigorous.

4. *Conclusions and recommendations.* Highlights (and lowlights) of the study bear repeating here to remind the reader of the study's goals,

to summarize how these goals were achieved, and to candidly discuss the study's limitations. The implications of the study findings are also important. How do these findings advance our knowledge? What are their applications to social work practice and policy? Finally, what are suggested directions for future research?

These four components represent an overview of how a qualitative report looks. For the reader who wishes to have a detailed description of the criteria of a good report, an excellent discussion can be found in Marshall and Rossman (1995).

CHOOSING A WRITING STANCE

Successful qualitative reports are written in an accessible prose style, and there are many acceptable ways to accomplish this. The eternal dilemma facing the qualitative researcher is how to balance critical distance with an appreciation of the respondents' humanity. The dangers lie in the extremes. A researcher who veers too far in the critical direction becomes an overzealous investigative reporter. The other extreme—ignoring or distorting the data to serve as an advocate—also erodes credibility.

In the belief that the best advocacy is built on a firm empirical foundation, I prefer the stance of the skeptic drawn from the social sciences (Lofland & Lofland, 1995) and the critical thinking approach (Gambrill, 1990). In the spirit of open inquiry, this mind-set is opposed to absolutist claims to authority and assertions that are unsupported. The skeptical mind-set is open, questioning, subjecting all claims to scrutiny. The best guardian against infallible claims based on cult-like faith in "higher authorities" is the critical thinker (Gambrill, 1990). Regardless of the amount of empathy we feel with our respondents, our responsibility lies in maintaining enough distance to place our findings in a larger, critical context. There may even be occasions when our report might offend our respondents or our own sense of loyalty to them.

A favorite tack in qualitative research writing is to *debunk*—to refute some cherished notion or to challenge the reader to think in new ways about a familiar phenomenon. Qualitative researchers are justifiably proud of their record of digging deep, of probing beneath the carefully constructed facade and coming up with findings that challenge the status quo. Carol Stack's (1974) study of African American women living in poverty struck home because she chronicled the resilience and resourcefulness of these women—a portrait that directly countered the "black family as pathology" viewpoint prevailing during the 1960s (and unfortunately continuing today). Similarly, many qualitative researchers embrace *irony* as a means of framing the findings (Lofland & Lofland, 1995), preferring to draw contrasts between what is received wisdom and what is observed, and delighting in the surprises of human nature that emerge from naturalistic inquiry.

Demystification is another motivating force in qualitative research, a force that threatens true believers who prefer ideology to critical reasoning. Describing the intricacies of human behavior takes in-depth probing and a willingness to be surprised and to be proven wrong. Reflexivity in the qualitative write-up is a form of demystification. When the report contains a candid description of the process of fieldwork—warts and all—the researcher's role and the methods of data collection and analysis are exposed for critical scrutiny.

Qualitative research is tailor-made for debunking, irony, and demystification. The politician who touts family values and privately abuses his wife, the mother who confesses to loathing her children as much as she loves them, and the "lazy" men on the street corner who are really furloughed construction workers (Liebow, 1967)—these are the stories that qualitative researchers delight in telling.

Qualitative reports also convey an insider's point of view that is missing from quantitative studies. Social work researchers can give voice to the powerless and oppressed—mothers on public assistance, incest survivors, the homeless, the elderly, gay and lesbian adolescents—groups whose voices are often silent or silenced in discussions about their welfare.

DEVELOPING A WRITING STYLE—METAPHORS, JARGON, AND (POST?) POSTMODERNISM

Finding the prose style you are most comfortable with takes time and practice. Whether you are an experienced writer or a novice, the act of writing up qualitative research requires decisions about form as well as content. Discussions about writing style have spawned a cottage industry of books about ethnographic writing (Agar, 1980; Atkinson, 1990; Clifford & Marcus, 1986; Emerson, Fretz, & Shaw, 1995; Geertz, 1988; Richardson, 1994; Wolcott, 1990; Van Maanen, 1988). Narrative styles gain ascendency, then lose favor in the climate of trendiness that surrounds academic and professional writing. Some qualitative researchers have advocated writing styles drawn from fiction, poetry, drama, and choreography (England, 1994; Janesick, 1994) as opposed to the traditional expository style of the social sciences. As with all other aspects of qualitative research, there is no one correct way to write a report.

Most successful qualitative reports have a rhythmic quality, weaving excerpts from the data into a seamless exposition of the study's themes and interpretation. They manifest originality of thought and creativity in conceptualization. They are knowledgeable and confident, but not pompous. They are compelling but not polemical. Whereas quantitative researchers present their findings in aggregate numerical form, qualitative researchers select and present "raw" data in the final report. Interposing excerpts such as vignettes and portions of narrative in the text certainly adds spice for the reader. But the purpose of excerpting is not only to vivify, but to inform.

The length of the excerpt depends on the approach taken by the researcher. Most qualitative studies juxtapose small chunks of data— verbatim quotes or brief vignettes—with presentations of conceptual themes and interpretation. Narrative analyses, on the other hand, use lengthy excerpts so that the narrative arc of the respondent's story can be presented intact. Of course, long narratives are no substitute for analysis and interpretation (Riessman, 1990).

Excerpts should push the overall narrative forward, not seem like a sideshow or a diversion. McCracken (1988) likened this process to a small plane practicing takeoffs and landings. The plane gains altitude (interpretation and exposition of study themes), but it also repeatedly touches down on the landing strip (excerpting of data). Flawless takeoffs and landings— moving easily from data to interpretation—are the goals of a successful write-up. In most qualitative reports, remember, too, that you are flying solo!

One of the more enjoyable aspects of writing (and reading) qualitative reports is the *use of metaphor.* Metaphors are rhetorical devices that paint word pictures. For example, Erving Goffman (1961) described the "careers" of mental patients and Sandelowski and Jones (1995) told of the "healing fictions" that pregnant women devise to explain the diagnosis of fetal anomalies. Each of these metaphors is evocative, providing imagery to guide us into a new way of looking at something.

Our respondents may themselves use metaphors. Their word pictures may be familiar and commonplace ("walking on thin ice") or they may be strikingly poetic. One of the women in our Mammogram Study, for example, said "I had a garden growing in my breast" to describe the presence of six tumors. The use of a gardening metaphor was also found by Mathews, Lannin, and Mitchell (1992) in their study of southern black women with metastatic breast cancer.

Other examples of metaphoric phrases include the following: Catherine Riessman (1990) wrote of the divorcing couple's "mourning of different dreams," Eliot Liebow (1993) described the daily traumas of homeless women as "little murders of everyday life," and Denise Burnette (1994) chronicled the "Sisyphus at work" quality of coping with chronic illness in old age.

Metaphors can also be used to describe the process of conducting qualitative research. In this book, I use the metaphor "journey of discovery" to describe qualitative inquiry. This phrase, for me, captures the excitement and uncertainty of qualitative research. Less uplifting (but no less graphic) is the "muddy boots" metaphor invoked by Schön (1983). In this word picture, scientists in their pristine white lab coats occupy the "high, hard ground" overlooking the swamp and qualitative researchers slog around in the swampy muck below. Although I find this contrast a bit overstated, it has served a purpose in provoking debate among qualitative researchers about their role vis-à-vis quantitative researchers (Ely et al., 1991; Guba & Lincoln, 1989).

Van Maanen (1988) used an old-fashioned post office as a metaphor to describe the analytic thinking that precedes some Realist Tales. Like the postal clerk, the ethnographer stands back from the data, stuffing bits and pieces of information into slots. The write-up is focused on the full slots, ignores the almost-empty slots, and goes through the mail bit by bit (p. 69). It is difficult to imagine a more dismissive (and effective) way to portray traditional modes of qualitative analysis.

A final word on prose style—try to *avoid jargon.* When use of technical jargon is absolutely necessary, explain its meaning to the reader. This is particularly important when using the terminology of qualitative methods—memoing, saturation, fieldwork, reflexivity, and so forth. Many qualitative researchers have adopted the language of postmodernism that has come to dominate much academic writing in recent years. Clifford Geertz (1973), an anthropologist who became an icon of the postmodern movement, urged ethnographers to pursue "thick description" and "inscription" in their research writing.

My concern is that "inscription" will (or has already) become "encryption"—giving rise to a style of writing impenetrable to all but a chosen few. Thus, issues are "problematized" and texts are "deconstructed" via "hermeneutic" approaches to root out sources of "hegemonic" bias that inhibit a "paradigm shift" away from positivism. Phenomenologists write about the "study of essences" and postmodernists decry "essentialist thinking." The nouns *privilege* and *foreground* have become verbs, and so on.

Those who embrace the new interpretive paradigms point to the capacity for language to reinforce an unjust status quo (Denzin & Lincoln, 1994). For example, feminist critiques have produced a greater awareness of the pervasiveness of masculinist bias in research writing. Similarly, the pro forma acceptance of a white, middle-class perspective in the social and behavioral sciences has been challenged by those who point to the ethnic and social class diversity of research "subjects." In this respect, the feminist and ethnic studies movements perform a valuable service in focusing attention on how oppression and inequality can be perpetuated in research.

Social work has not been immune to these trends. Some social work researchers proposed using narrative methods (Cohler, 1994; Riessman, 1993; Tobin, 1994), discourse analysis (Chambon & Irving, 1994; Sherman, 1994), feminist critiques (Swigonski, 1994) and heuristic approaches (Pieper, 1989; Tyson, 1994) as alternatives to positivistic styles of research and writing. Of course, use of such approaches need not entail using postmodern (or even post-postmodern) jargon. Nor is jargon solely a problem in postmodernist writing. Its stultifying effects can be found in any number of research reports—quantitative as well as qualitative.

THE ROLE OF SOCIAL WORK VALUES—HUMAN AGENCY AND THE STRENGTHS PERSPECTIVE

Although a discussion of social work values could fit into any chapter of this book, I chose to place it in the context of the write-up because it is here that such values can be made most explicit to the reader. Social work research is humanistic and reformist in nature, regardless of whether it is quantitative or qualitative. One means of expressing these values is to stress human agency and a strengths perspective to counterbalance the pathological approach that underlies many clinical theories (Schein, 1987).

Human agency refers to the capacity of human beings to be active and resourceful rather than passive pawns of social forces. In qualitative social work research, a concern for human agency is manifested in the way we observe human actions, in the questions we ask, and in the way we frame and present our findings. (Of course, we do not manufacture strengths if they do not exist.)

Qualitative research has no inherent capacity for bringing about reform and can be just as nonreformist as any quantitative study. There are plenty of monographs that exemplify the wonders of thick description without a hint of concern for social justice. But the argument can also be made that a natural affinity exists between the humanistic perspectives of naturalistic inquiry and the concerns of advocates for the disadvantaged.

The challenge of combining a strengths perspective (describing what is) with concern for social inequality (advocating for what should be) is an ongoing dilemma for social work. On the one hand, a report emphasizing strengths plays into the hands of conservatives who delight in hearing how well the poor and disadvantaged are doing. On the other hand, a reformist report spotlights problems to challenge the status quo, thereby reinforcing the pathology viewpoint.

Social work researchers share with their practitioner colleagues the strengths versus social change dilemma. Let us revisit the earlier hypothetical study of mentally disabled persons coping with cutbacks in their SSI benefits. When writing up the study, we might emphasize the resilience of the respondents, how they seek assistance from family and friends and survive this tremendous financial stress. But one might also use case histories of troubled SSI recipients living in fear of eviction as the focus of the study. In this way, the report can become part of a public advocacy campaign to reverse the cuts in SSI.

Is it possible to resolve this dilemma by describing strengths as well as problems in the final report? I believe this can be done. But it requires a delicate balancing act, juggling rich description of "what is" with a compelling argument that social conditions must be changed.

And if the empirical findings conflict with our reformist goals? Regardless of the outcome, we tell the story. The temptation to distort data and mislead, even for noble purposes, should be resisted. We may make a strong case as advocates, but we then forever lose credibility as researchers.

THE ULTIMATE GOAL—DISSEMINATION OF THE STUDY FINDINGS

Dissemination is the ultimate goal of all research—all is for naught if the work is not somehow made available to a wider audience. Researchers have a number of reasons (excuses?) for not disseminating. We may set unrealistic standards for our work and then put it on a shelf to collect dust until we can revise it to meet these standards—a surefire recipe for neglect. Then there is fear of failure. As Robert Weiss (1994) noted, "writing is exposure" (p. 205). To this I would add that submitting reports for publication is one of the more humbling experiences of being a researcher.

The process of publishing research findings in a world ruled by social Darwinist editorial boards can be intimidating. By social Darwinism, I am referring to the sifting and sorting process where the "fittest" of the studies "survives" to be published or selected for a conference presentation. The determination of "fitness" may be based on merit or laden with bias. In spite of these hurdles, fear of failure is not a sufficient excuse for avoiding the effort to disseminate.

There are three basic avenues to disseminate qualitative studies: oral presentations, books, and journal articles. The qualitative researcher can consider any one or all of these. *Oral presentation* of the study findings at conferences, workshops, and seminars is perhaps the most easily accessible mode of dissemination.

Qualitative reports are especially suited for publication as *books* because they tend to be lengthy. Most of the "classic" works in ethnography and sociology were originally released in book form. Regrettably, the days when academic presses offered small press runs of scholarly books are virtually over. Our most cherished findings may not hold up in the market-driven competition for sale-worthiness.

Writing up qualitative research for *peer-reviewed journal publication* is probably the most challenging means of dissemination for two reasons. First of all, squeezing qualitative findings into 25 or fewer pages without compromising their integrity is difficult to pull off. This may partly explain the scarcity of qualitative studies in academic journals (Fraser, 1994). Some qualitative researchers cannot bear to compress so much effort into a few pages and thus avoid journals altogether.

Second, whereas there is obvious variation in difficulty level, peer-reviewed journals tend to have standards that are hard to meet. Given the high rejection rates of the leading journals, many researchers undoubtedly give up before they start.

I believe that this self-screening is unnecessary and self-defeating. Unless explicitly told not to resubmit, I consider rejection letters with reviewers' comments enclosed as open invitations to try again. (I learned this lesson from a more experienced colleague who congratulated me when I dejectedly showed him my first rejection letter from a journal editor.) More often, I am told I may revise and resubmit with no guarantee of publication, which I do (assuming the suggested revisions are reasonable). In fact, I have never had a manuscript accepted *without* having to do revisions. I would be suspicious of the quality of the journal if I did! Even if you are firmly rejected by a journal, peer reviewers' comments usually offer helpful tips for revising and resubmitting the manuscript elsewhere. As difficult as it may seem at first, the development of a thick skin and unabashed willingness to revise and resubmit is the best survival mechanism around.

Getting qualitative studies published in a quantitative world is an ongoing struggle. There are fewer journals willing to publish qualitative research and too few reviewers available with expertise in qualitative methodology. Many journal editors and reviewers are unfamiliar with the conventions of qualitative methods and are ill-prepared to evaluate their merit. As more and more qualitative studies are produced, the stage is set for a tremendous bottleneck in reviewing and publishing qualitative studies in journals.

Even when journal editors and reviewers are favorably disposed toward qualitative studies, the absence of consensual standards for quality opens the door to arbitrariness. Unlike quantitative research where standards for quality control are known and generally agreed on, qualitative studies are more likely to be subject to the whims of editors or reviewers. When guidelines are diverse and ever changing, dissemination is made more difficult.

All of these difficulties associated with publishing qualitative studies in peer-reviewed journals raise serious concerns for professionals and academics seeking scholarly recognition, as peer-reviewed publications are the most valued forums of scholarly achievement. I know of no easy answers to this dilemma except to argue for more tolerance and under-standing—and more rigorous qualitative research—so that these barriers can be overcome.

Finally, there are newly developing routes of dissemination via electronic media. The growing availability of on-line chat groups, journals, and Web sites has made electronic presentations of qualitative research possible through the Internet and other on-line media. For example, Ronald Chenail of Nova Southeastern University in Florida has produced an on-line journal entitled *The Qualitative Report* that is accessible to anyone on the World Wide Web—http://www.nova.edu/ssss/QR. This route to dissemination will undoubtedly grow in the future.

SUMMARY AND CONCLUSION

This chapter has offered a number of suggestions for framing the qualitative research report, including targeting one's audience and situat-ing the study along the continua of diachronic versus synchronic, emic versus etic, and reflexive versus nonreflexive. Not the least of these considerations is the choice of writing style, as the readability of a qualitative report is an essential element of its success.

Every well-conducted qualitative study has a home somewhere out there, even if it is in a relatively obscure journal or on the program of a small-scale conference. What is most important is that we make the effort at dissemination—our scholarly responsibilities require no less of us.

CODA: SOME EXEMPLARY
MONOGRAPHS FOR ADDITIONAL READING

Becker, H., Geer, B., Hughes, E., & Strauss, A. (1961). *Boys in white: Student culture in medical school.* Chicago: University of Chicago Press.

Bosk, C. L. (1979). *Forgive and remember: Managing medical failure.* Chicago: University of Chicago Press.

Bourgois, P. (1995). *In search of respect: Selling crack in El Barrio.* New York: Cambridge University Press.

Duneier, M. (1992). *Slim's table: Race, respectability, and masculinity.* Chicago: University of Chicago Press.

Estroff, S. (1981). *Making it crazy.* Berkeley: University of California Press.

Goffman, E. (1961). *Asylums: Essays on the social situation of mental patients and other inmates.* Garden City, NY: Basic Books.

Hochschild, A. (1983). *The managed heart: Commercialization of human feeling.* Berkeley: University of California Press.

Hochschild, A. (with Machung, A.). (1989). *The second shift: Inside the two-job marriage.* New York: Avon.

Humphries, L. (1970). *Tearoom trade: Impersonal sex in public places.* Chicago:Aldine.

Liebow, E. (1967). *Talley's corner: A study of Negro street corner men.* Boston: Little, Brown.

Liebow, E. (1993). *Tell them who I am: The lives of homeless women.* New York: Penguin.

Lynd, R. S. & Lynd, H. M. (1956). *Middletown: A study in modern American culture.* New York: Harcourt Brace.

Myerhoff, B. (1978). *Number our days: A triumph of continuity and culture among Jewish old people in an urban ghetto.* New York: Simon & Schuster.

Norman, E. (1990). *Women at war: The story of fifty military nurses who served in Vietnam.* Philadelphia: University of Pennsylvania Press.

Painter, N. I. (1979). *The narrative of Hosea Hudson: His life as a Negro communist in the south.* Cambridge, MA: Harvard University Press.

Powdermaker, H. (1966). *Stranger and friend: The way of an anthropologist.* New York: Norton.

Riessman, C. K. (1990). *Divorce talk.* New Brunswick, NJ: Rutgers University Press.

Stack, C. (1974). *All our kin. Strategies for survival in a black community.* New York: Harper Colophon.

Stack, C. (1996). *Call to home: The return migration of African-Americans to the South.* New York: Basic Books.

Whyte, W. F. (1955). *Street corner society* (2nd ed.). Chicago: University of Chicago Press.

Chapter 10

MULTIMETHOD RESEARCH
The Synergy of Combining Qualitative and Quantitative Methods

The previous chapters in this book were directed to those who wish to carry out "purely" qualitative research—studies that can proudly stand alone as rigorous and relevant contributions to building knowledge. In this chapter, I will describe ways to highlight the strengths (and offset many of the weaknesses) of quantitative and qualitative methods as part of a multi-method approach. Although requiring some compromises along the way, pursuing this strategy gives us the opportunity to enjoy the best of both worlds.

BACKGROUND

Support for the multimethod approach has come from both quantitative and qualitative researchers, including foremost proponents of experimental and quasi-experimental designs (Campbell & Stanley, 1963; Cook & Campbell, 1979) as well as the founders of grounded theory (Glaser & Strauss, 1967) and other qualitative researchers in education, nursing, and family medicine (Bryman, 1988; Cook & Reichardt, 1979; Creswell, 1994; Firestone, 1990; Howe, 1988; Jick, 1983; Morse, 1991; Patton, 1986, 1990; Salomon, 1991; Stange, Miller, Crabtree, O'Connor, & Zyzanski, 1994). Many social work researchers share this sentiment as well (Bernstein &

Epstein, 1994; Blake, 1989; Combs-Orme, 1990; I. Davis, 1994; Fortune, 1990; Glisson, 1990; Grinnell, 1997; Harrison, 1994; Hartman, 1994; Toseland, 1994).

Despite such widespread endorsement, surprisingly few multimethod studies can be found in the literature. There are several likely explanations for this. First, researchers are usually trained in one or the other methodology, but not both. Even in disciplines with strong traditions in both methods (e.g., sociology), there are two camps with sporadic outbreaks of antipathy between them (Feagin et al., 1991).

Second, there is considerable confusion over which components of the methods can be integrated, starting with epistemologies (positivist, constructivist, feminist, postmodern, etc.) and continuing with research designs, data collection, data analysis, and write-up. Once the thorny dilemma of epistemological compatibility is resolved, the process of integration usually proceeds much more smoothly (Allen-Meares, 1995; Haase & Myers, 1988; Stern, 1994).

A final reason for the scarcity of multimethod studies is logistical. Multimethod studies require dual competencies and considerable outlays of time and resources. It is almost always easier for qualitative and quantitative researchers to follow separate paths, even when multimethod studies are clearly the superior route to take.

Returning to the issue of epistemological compatibility, the most vocal opponents of multimethod collaboration reside in one corner of the qualitative camp. (Quantitative researchers who reject the multimethod approach probably see less need to speak up because they belong to the dominant camp and can simply ignore the issue.) Paradigm purists argue that the fallacy of an "objective truth" or "reality" apart from subjective interpretation cannot peacefully coexist with a critique built on the subjective and ephemeral nature of reality (Ely et al., 1991; Greene, 1994). Whereas some seek mutual tolerance and less "shouting across the rift" (Ely et al., 1991, p. 216), others take pride in denouncing the scientific methods of the Eurocentric, patriarchical establishment and prefer to press on with the rhetoric of rejection (Denzin & Lincoln, 1994; Greene, 1994). Some clinicians have also joined the fray, decrying the privileged status of scientists and the methods that give short shrift to the messy world of clinical practice with the poor and underserved (Imre, 1990; Meyer, 1990; Schön, 1983; Siporin, 1988; Wood, 1990).

The dismissive and condescending attitudes of some quantitative researchers have not helped matters. Having firsthand experience with the frustration of dealing with these naysayers, I can sympathize with my colleagues who adopt an epistemology more closely aligned with their feminist, postmodern, or constructivist inclinations.

But I cannot join them. To be sure, there are limits to what positivism and the scientific method can do for us. But I am not ready to reject the quantitative world, nor do I believe such a stance is good for social work research. Qualitative research can open new doors of knowledge and provide the richest of experiences, but it is not a substitute for quantitative methods. Although inclined to wish for equity in the qualitative-quantitative mix, I am too much the pragmatist to suggest throwing quantitative methods out with the bathwater.

THREE MODES OF
MULTIMETHOD RESEARCH

The combining of qualitative and quantitative methods can take three basic forms—two involve temporal sequencing and the third entails concurrent use of the methods at the same time and within the same study (Creswell, 1994). By temporal sequencing, I am referring to conducting a qualitative study first, followed by a quantitative study, or vice versa.

A caveat before we begin: This classification of types of multimethod studies is offered primarily as a heuristic device. In reality, most multimethod studies are better described as existing along a continuum rather than fitting neatly into a categorical type. The location of a study on the quantitative-qualitative continuum can also shift over time.

The Qual→Quant Mode

Using the shorthand notation of Creswell (1994), the first type of multimethod combination can be depicted as QUAL→QUANT. Here, the qualitative study comes first, typically an "exploratory" study in which concepts and potential hypotheses are identified via observation and open-ended interviews with individuals or focus groups. In the second stage of the study, concepts derived from the qualitative analyses are operationalized and hypotheses are tested with quantitative techniques.

The QUAL→QUANT approach is particularly useful for researchers who are developing multi-item scales to measure a phenomenon. For example, social work clinician Peggy MacGregor (1994) wrote about grief-like reactions among parents whose children are diagnosed with schizophrenia, a phenomenon that was also observed by Phyllis Vine (1982) in her ethnographic study of families of persons with severe mental illness. These observations, in turn, led Vine, Struening, and other colleagues at New York State Psychiatric Institute to develop and psychometrically test a Grief Scale for assessing families of persons with severe mental illness (Struening et al., 1995). The quantitative analyses of the Grief Scale revealed a useful instrument for further studies of the stresses (and rewards) of caregiving for a relative with serious mental illness (Struening et al., 1995).

The validity of concepts and hypotheses in quantitative research is enhanced enormously by grounding them in "real world" observations. Regardless of whom you want to study—sex offenders, asthma patients, or circus clowns—it is sensible to start by speaking with them at length and with an open mind.

The Quant→Qual Mode

In the second type of multimethod research (QUANT→QUAL), the findings of a quantitative study are the departure point for a qualitative study. In her study of the impact of culture on clinical practice, Eva Lu (1994) found statistically significant differences between Asian and non-Asian American psychotherapists on the Achieving Styles Inventory ([ASI]; Lipman-Blumen, 1987) that indicated a more collaborative and less controlling style of interaction among the Asian American clinicians. These findings led Dr. Lu (1996) to pursue in-depth interviews with eight Asian and non-Asian social work clinicians to discuss their therapeutic approaches to assessment and treatment when presented with a case vignette of a troubled Asian American family. In this way, the quantitative findings of differential scores on the ASI were extended and deepened to reveal how the cultural background of the clinician can affect clinical judgment.

Many a quantitative study could benefit from post hoc qualitative inquiry of questions left unanswered (and unanswerable) by quantitative analyses. Researchers in the social sciences have reason to be humble when intepreting findings, as causal factors are invariably numerous and difficult to capture in hypothetico-deductive conceptual frameworks. One need only point to the modest "R squares" of most multiple regression analyses in the social science literature to illustrate the limits of many conceptual models in accounting for variance in the dependent variable—usually some important behavioral, cognitive, or affective outcome.

The Quant↔Qual Mode

The third type of multimethod approach (QUANT↔QUAL) integrates qualitative and quantitative methods concurrently within the same study. One method may be dominant over the other (QUANT-qual or QUAL-quant) or the two methods may be given equal weight throughout the research process. In the "dominant-less dominant" designs, one approach becomes nested within a dominant study design (Creswell, 1994). Perhaps not surprisingly, the research literature contains many more examples of nested studies than of fully integrated studies. It is easier to give one approach a dominant role than to aim for a partnership of equals.

When following the QUANT-qual model, researchers typically collect qualitative data and enliven their quantitative findings by presenting case vignettes. Or they may present excerpts from responses to open-ended questions in addition to the findings from analyses of data from a standardized interview (Morgan, 1988). In these instances, the use of qualitative data to supplement quantitative findings does not significantly change the quantitative thrust of the study.

In the QUAL-quant approach, qualitative researchers include survey, census, and Likert-scale data along with qualitative data. Snow and Anderson (1991), for example, made use of tracking data from various agencies to supplement their intensive interviews and ethnographic observation of the homeless. The resulting depiction of the lives of the homeless contained both statistical as well as ethnographic descriptions of their lives.

In another manifestation of the QUAL-quant model, qualitative researchers include standardized measurement scales as part of their interviews and report the quantitative findings from these measures. If, for example, you are interested in learning about the experiences of war refugees, you may wish to measure their level of post-traumatic stress symptomatology to assess their psychological status (and also to identify those who may need referrals to counseling). Using quantitative data in this manner need not detract from the inductive, emergent nature of the qualitative study.

INTEGRATED OR MIXED-MODEL STUDIES

The most challenging type of multimethod research is the fully integrated (QUAL↔QUANT) approach. Here, quantitative and qualitative methods are given equal weight at all (or at least most) stages of the study. Optimally, researchers using this model have solid expertise in both qualitative and quantitative methods and a willingness to compromise in transversing paradigms (Haase & Myers, 1988). Because many researchers do not possess the former and are unwilling to do the latter, the mixed model remains a rarity.

Figure 10.1 offers a concept map of how a mixed-method study might unfold over time. Starting at the beginning, we provide a rationale for including both approaches so that the reader can understand their respective and complementary goals.

In describing the objectives of the study, the researcher includes both rich description as well as tests of relationships and comparisons of group differences. Literature reviews typically take different forms in quantitative and qualitative studies, but a middle ground can usually be found. When reviewing the theoretical and empirical literature, quantitative researchers can "loosen" the thread of their arguments, leaving more room for new concepts to emerge and for qualitative findings to challenge existing theories and explanatory frameworks. By the same token, qualitative researchers can accept a review of the literature organized around key concepts or variables.

During the design and implementation stages of an integrated study, qualitative researchers may have to accommodate to a more linear approach, because it is difficult to maintain the iterative stance of moving back and forth between design, sampling, data collection, and data analysis. Nevertheless, some degree of flexibility can be built into the study to allow for changes and adjustments.

In sampling respondents, multiple approaches may be used, drawing on probability sampling associated with quantitative methods as well as purposive (or snowball) sampling favored by qualitative researchers. Parallel forms of data collection—standardized interviews or questionnaires combined with observation or unstructured interviews—provide a mix of quantitative and qualitative data that are then analyzed and interpreted to yield statistical findings as well as codes and themes (see Figure 10.1).

The write-up of an integrated study usually presents the two sets of findings in a compartmentalized fashion where statistical findings and codes or themes are presented side by side. Ideally, the findings are interwoven together into a synthesis—the whole becoming greater than the parts. There are three likely outcomes when one chooses to integrate

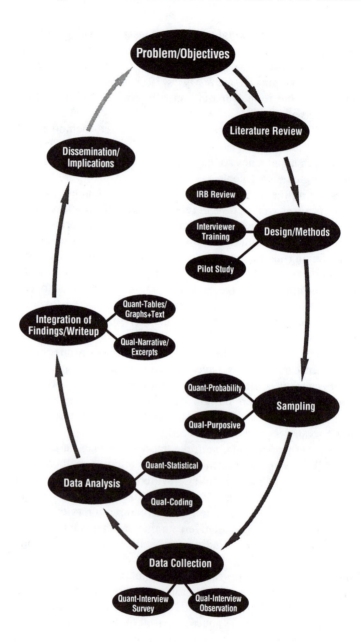

Figure 10.1. Concept Map of an Integrated Qualitative-Quantitative Study

qualitative and quantitative findings: (a) the findings converge with each other (i.e., triangulation is successfully achieved); (b) the findings complement each other (i.e., they differ but do not conflict); and (c) the findings contradict each other.

Here is a hypothetical example: Let us say that fear of cancer emerges as a major theme from the qualitative interviews in our Mammogram Study and the quantitative analyses reveal that one of the strongest predictors of delay is fear of cancer (measured quantitatively by a scale score). In this case, we have triangulated findings and can feel relatively confident that fear is a major (although not necessarily only) contributor to delay.

But our qualitative interviews may also reveal a more nuanced view of our respondents' feelings about breast cancer. Perhaps fear of cancer is mentioned in the interviews, but other life stresses are just as prominent (or more prominent) in these women's lives (e.g., one of our respondents was grieving the recent death of her son, another was struggling with diabetic complications, another faced eviction from her apartment, etc.). In this case, the qualitative findings give depth and expanded meaning to the quantitative findings without directly conflicting with them.

Multimethod studies get especially interesting when the qualitative findings and quantitative findings contradict one another. There is no convergence or complimentarity, just puzzling discrepancies. When this happens, we must examine both sets of findings closely. If both appear to be valid, we may report them as such and let the reader decide which carries more weight.

Continuing with the hypothetical example from our Mammogram Study, let us say that fear of cancer is an important theme from the qualitative interviews, but its scale score is a very weak predictor in the multiple regression analyses. Rather than try to reconcile this seeming discrepancy, we would be wise to simply report it (and call for more studies of fear of cancer and its impact on follow-up behaviors).

Mixed-method studies require more than epistemological compromises. For those of us who prefer to follow the venerable tradition of the Lone Ethnographer, we must learn to work in a team—an activity our quantitative colleagues have already become accustomed to. It is hard to imagine how one person could carry out all phases of a multimethod study. Our Mammogram Study team includes two interviewers (one of whom also functions as Project Director and Data Manager), two transcribers, a statistician, a medical-records auditor, and four coprincipal investigators. (None of the team members works on the study full time.) Our study is admittedly subsidized by federal funding, but we could not have carried it out without such financial support. I estimate that transcribing and coding of the qualitative data (which includes regular meetings to discuss the codes and use of computers to organize the coding) take four to five times longer than the quantitative data entry and analyses require.

Whereas quantitative researchers must be patient and adjust their time lines to accommodate qualitative analysis, qualitative researchers have to cut back in other ways to conserve resources and coordinate timing with the quantitative side. Because we do not wish to cut corners in data analysis, we often limit the scope of data collection, which usually means less time spent in observation.

Given the creative tension involved in coordinating two different modes of inquiry, the temptation to revert to a dominant-less dominant design is ever present. (More often than not, the quantitative side comes out ahead in these situations.) Maintaining a balance between the qualitative and quantitative within the confines of the same study takes good faith and constant vigilance.

Despite its demands, the mixed-method approach is worth the effort. When both methods are given their due, a study can be enhanced greatly by their synergy. Social work research is especially fertile ground for these types of studies, because we are interested in quantitative assessments of needs and outcomes as well as qualitative understanding of the lives of clients.

MULTIMETHOD APPROACHES
TO PROGRAM AND PRACTICE EVALUATION

As discussed in Chapter 1, qualitative methods are well suited to program evaluation, but they are problematic when conducted in practice by the practitioner. However, qualitative evaluations *in* clinical practice should not be confused with evaluations *of* practice. The latter approach maintains a strict separation of the roles of clinician and researcher, thereby allowing each to carry out his or her respective mandates.

Qualitative evaluators use the same methods of data collection and analysis as other qualitative researchers. However, qualitative program evaluation differs from nonevaluative research in one important respect— its inherently social and political nature. From conception to completion, program evaluations are immersed in a sea of policy implications and competing interests.

In a fundamental sense, evaluation is "finding the value" (Ruckdeschel, Earnshaw, & Firrek, 1994; Scriven, 1967), making judgments according to societal priorities. Evaluation researchers must work under constraints of time, resources, and competing ideas regarding what is of "value." Even when vested interest groups—policymakers, administrators, staff, clients—generally agree on a program's goals, the evaluator must work under close scrutiny and risk offending one or another of the stakeholders.

A number of qualitative researchers have advocated applying the multimethod approach to educational evaluation (Brewer & Hunter, 1989; Cook & Reichardt, 1979; Jick, 1983; Patton, 1990; Salomon, 1991) and to evaluation of social work practice (Bernstein & Epstein, 1994; I. Davis, 1994; Harrison, 1994). Arguments that the legitimacy and credibility of social work practice depend on its demonstrated effectiveness (Fischer, 1973; Myers & Thyer, 1997; Reid, 1994; Thyer, 1996) lay the groundwork for multimethod evaluations of social work practice and social welfare programs. Social work educators and researchers who elevate practice wisdom over systematic evaluation will find that colleagues in psychiatry, psychology, and nursing are more than willing to empirically assess the effectiveness of their interventions.

Even the bastions of traditional social work practice—child and family protective services—have come under intense pressure to prove their effectiveness. Media reports of severe, even fatal, child abuse have multiplied dramatically in recent years amid a public outcry over ineffective agencies and poorly trained staff. Many practitioners and agency administrators applaud efforts to increase accountability and have begun to systematically gather data to track children and families at risk and evaluate program and treatment outcomes.

The same issues in the general debate over qualitative versus quantitative paradigms arise in discussions of multimethod evaluation. Qualitative researchers who are philosophically opposed to quantitative methods (and therefore to multimethod approaches) argue that these methods have taught us very little about how and why programs work (Greene, 1994; House, 1980; Scriven, 1967; Weiss, 1987). Other dissenters in the qualitative camp draw on the familiar argument that the "objectivist" and "subjectivist" paradigms do not mix (Guba & Lincoln, 1981, 1990).

For those willing to collaborate, there are several ways that qualitative researchers can contribute to program evaluation in a multimethod approach. Quantitative evaluations are good at establishing *what* works, but qualitative evaluations help us understand *how* a program succeeds or fails. Although admittedly more time consuming, qualitative methods are less intrusive and less demanding on the agency than an experimental trial. Qualitative researchers can fade into the woodwork and respond flexibly to the ebb and flow of organizational life. The addition of qualitative methods to a quantitative evaluation adds flexibility and depth (Drake et al., 1993).

As mentioned in Chapter 1, qualitative research is particularly well suited to studies of *process*—probing the black box for subtle facets of program implementation that elude quantitative measurement (Dehar et al., 1993). The "fidelity" of a program or a treatment—its adherence to a specified set of goals and procedures—is especially amenable to qualitative inquiry (Blakely et al., 1987).The nuances of social programs—the dynamic interplay of the actors, their differing perceptions of events, the effects of culture and gender—are difficult to anticipate and measure (Drake et al., 1993).

Qualitative approaches also mesh well with social work values— they empower less powerful stakeholders (clients, lower level staff, etc.) by giving their voices greater prominence in "finding the value" of the program. A multimethod approach cannot guarantee a successful evaluation, but it will invariably enhance the depth and relevance of the findings.

Let us take the example of a "paradigm shifting" program known as Pathways to Housing, a nonprofit agency founded in 1992 to serve the homeless mentally ill in New York City. Long considered the most difficult population to engage and treat effectively, homeless mentally ill clients of Pathways to Housing have shown a remarkable ability to adapt successfully to independent living when provided immediate housing with no strings attached.

This is where the paradigm shift is most evident—Pathways clients can make use of a variety of case management services, but their right to housing is not linked to use of these services. The requirements of the "continuum of care" model—medication compliance, sobriety, and a myriad of residential treatment "house" rules—do not apply (Tsemberis, 1997). Nor are there any limits on "length of stay"; clients may reside in their apartments as long as needed. In contrast, the traditional paradigm of psychiatric rehabilitation precludes accepting clients who are medication noncompliant, dually diagnosed (with substance abuse problems), or have histories of arrests or violent behavior.

The philosophy and goals of the Pathways to Housing program render it a good example of the "new paradigm" in services for the homeless mentally ill, an approach favoring client choice and autonomy (Carling, 1993; Ridgway & Zipple, 1990). The program is also an excellent candidate for multimethod evaluation, because many providers and policymakers are skeptical that such programs can succeed (Hatfield, 1993; Lamb & Lamb, 1990).

To facilitate evaluation, a team composed of Pathways staff and researchers has developed a database-management system to monitor clients' progress in attaining certain goals such as housing stability, linkages to services and the community, and overall quality of life. Both quantitative measures (administered by case managers) and qualitative assessment (carried out by an ethnographer and trained interviewers) are used to record data on the client's status.

In addition to assessing individual outcomes through qualitative and quantitative data collection and case manager reports, the staff-research team at Pathways has designed an experimental evaluation of the program in which eligible clients are randomly assigned to receive Pathways services or the usual continuum of care services. (As the program currently has a waiting list that exceeds its capacity, it is ethically acceptable to assign clients to a control group and compare process and outcomes for the two groups). Although case managers report marked improvements in clients' functioning (with only a few program dropouts among more than 200 clients served since 1992), the multimethod experimental design will provide more formal evidence of the program's achievements. In this way, the new paradigm will be supported (or refuted) by the best available empirical evidence.

Evaluating Clinical Practice:
Looking Into the Black Box

Quantitative evaluations of various treatment modalities have involved quasi-experimental single-system designs as well as experimental group designs. For example, controlled trials have demonstrated the efficacy of cognitive behavioral treatment for depression, panic disorder, obsessive-compulsive disorder, borderline personality disorder, and eating disorders (Elkin et al., 1989; Goisman, 1997; Linehan, Armstrong, Suarez, Allmon, & Heard, 1991; Myers & Thyer, 1997). Social work researchers have collaborated in documenting the success of Assertive Community Treatment for schizophrenia (Burns & Santos, 1995; Stein & Test, 1980), psychoeducation for families of persons with schizophrenia (Hogarty et al., 1986; McFarlane et al., 1994), and task-centered practice approaches (Reid, 1994).

The use of qualitative methods—either alone or as part of a multimethod approach—is relatively rare in evaluations of clinical practice, especially psychotherapeutic practice. Dating back to the 1940s, the field of psychotherapy research has been dominated by psychologists who used quantified measures of treatment process and outcomes to demonstrate the effectiveness of diverse psychotherapeutic modalities (Orlinsky, 1994). As a result, psychotherapy has been termed "the best documented medical intervention in history" (Maling & Howard, 1994, p. 247).

Although still overwhelmingly quantitative, the field of psychotherapy research has had a growing number of proponents of the "qualitative alternative" in recent years (Stiles, 1994, p. 158). Here, the black box consists of the "how" questions surrounding psychotherapy—how the therapeutic alliance forms, how therapists and clients perceive the alliance, how sociocultural factors affect (or impede) the therapist-client relationship, and so forth.

Thus far, qualitative psychotherapy research has pursued a line of inquiry that is a difficult fit for multimethod collaboration and evaluation, focusing on *discourse analysis* as well as *interpretivist, narrative approaches* (Bruner, 1987; Mishler, 1986; Polkinghorne, 1988; Riessman, 1993; Sarbin, 1986; Schafer, 1992; Spence, 1982; Stiles, 1994). Some narrative analyses of "master stories" draw on a long psychodynamic tradition of encouraging clients to derive insight by framing their experiences in their own words (Edelson, 1994; Teller & Dahl, 1986). Other forms of narrative analysis use a Talmudic-like examination of transcripts based on techniques developed by linguists (Labov & Waletzky, 1967; Mishler, 1986; Riessman, 1993).

Narrative analyses of the "poetic structures" of respondents' accounts of their lives are intrinsically interesting, but they risk omitting an important dimension of qualitative inquiry—observation and interpretation of the client beyond the clinical encounter (Laird, 1994; Riessman, 1993). As one critic said of Labov's techniques, "his assumption [is] that narrative is a relation among clauses rather than an interaction among participants" (Langellier, 1989, p. 248). Put another way, narrative analysis elevates text over context. Even its proponents admit that it takes "some fancy epistemological footwork" to make narrative analysis fit with other types of qualitative and quantitative methods (Riessman, 1993, p. 70).

Compared to program evaluation, practice evaluation is a decidedly low-tech enterprise, fueled more by dedication than by funding or policy imperatives. Unfettered (but also underfunded), evaluations of practice are more likely to be done by a lone practitioner or researcher than by a team monitoring qualitative and quantitative indicators of process and outcome.

Yet, qualitative methods are entirely appropriate for multimethod evaluations *of* clinical practice. For example, the qualitative researcher could conduct in-depth interviews with clients, family members, and therapists, observe and take fieldnotes on the clinical encounter, and do content analyses of case files and process recordings. Perhaps the not-too-distant future will bring an epistemological rapprochement between quantitative and qualitative methods so that multimethod evaluations of practice can become more common.

SUMMARY AND FINAL CONCLUSION

Multimethod approaches can bring us the best of both worlds, but their promise remains largely unfulfilled. A number of epistemological and methodological barriers stand in the way of integrating quantitative and qualitative approaches, not the least of which are the additional outlays of expertise, time, and resources required.

Despite the protestations of paradigm purists, both sides can benefit from collaboration. However, the acceptance of multimethod research depends in part on the success of qualitative researchers in making their case that qualitative inquiry is a valuable and trustworthy enterprise.

Which brings me full circle to my primary reason for writing this book. Qualitative studies have intrinsic appeal to professionals and to lay audiences alike. Unfortunately, they are not taken seriously enough in the places that matter. The challenge comes from living in a world full of skeptics quite ready to dismiss qualitative methods as "soft" subjectivity, easy to do and irrelevant to the important issues of the day.

Qualitative researchers have responded to this challenge in varying ways, reflecting the profound diversity within the qualitative family. Some ignore the challenge, believing that the mystique of qualitative methods transcends such an unenlightened attitude. Others choose rejection and retreat from the quantitative world.

I can offer no empirical evidence to support this contention but here goes anyway: I believe that the vast majority of qualitative researchers want to engage with the quantitative world, relying on actions, not just words, to assert the value of naturalistic inquiry. This is admittedly a tall order, an agenda that places far more of the burden of proof on qualitative researchers than on their quantitative brethren.

Whether monomethod or multimethod in approach, qualitative studies in social work research should abide by the "three R's"—Rigor, Relevance, and (social) Responsibility. To be done well, they take a certain type of person (persistent, sensitive, and well armed with a sense of humor). And they take large quantities of time and energy—emotional as well as intellectual.

It is by producing rigorous, relevant, and responsible qualitative research that we will make our case. Qualitative research is laborious, but it is also a labor of love. We need only go forth and do it well.

Epilogue

QUALITATIVE METHODS IN SOCIAL WORK EDUCATION
Toward Developing an Infrastructure

With nary a dissenting voice, the chorus of support for qualitative methods in social work education has swelled in recent years. This endorsement extends to the professional organizations representing social work educators—the Council on Social Work Education (CSWE), the National Association of Deans and Directors of Schools of Social Work, the Group for the Advancement of Doctoral Education (GADE), and the Association of Baccalaureate Program Directors. Official reports from organizations representing social work researchers (GADE, 1992; Task Force on Social Work Research, 1991) recommend qualitative as well as quantitative methods as part of the research curricula required of social work students. Although far from achieving parity with quantitative methods in representation, research textbooks and social work journals are giving more prominence to qualitative methods and to qualitative studies.

Some of the strongest support for qualitative research has come from clinicians working in the psychotherapeutic tradition that influenced much of social work practice by the 1980s (L. V. Davis, 1994; Goldstein, 1981; Heineman-Pieper, 1981; Rodwell, 1987; Saleeby, 1989; Siporin, 1988). From their perspective, quantitative methods are ill suited to the world of practice because they are reductionistic, decontextualizing, and dehumanizing. This trend in clinical social work paralleled postpositivist and social constructionist movements in psychology (Gergen, 1985), feminist theory (Reinharz, 1992), and the humanities (Denzin & Lincoln, 1994).

The clash of epistemologies precipitated by criticism of scientific methods led to a prolonged and acrimonious debate that consumed much space in the social work literature; for a sampling see books by Videka-Sherman and Reid (1990), Sherman & Reid (1994), Riessman (1994), Hudson and Nurius (1994), and Tyson (1995), as well as the March 1993 edition of *Social Service Review* and the March 1995 edition of *Social Work Research.* The debate pitted critics of logical positivism (not all of whom were qualitative researchers) against defenders of quantitative methods (some of whom *were* qualitative researchers). Although it has calmed down a bit, the epistemology debate simmers along, drawing sustenance from the unfortunate divide between research and practice that afflicts social work as well as other clinical professions.

For those content with "many ways of knowing" (Hartman, 1994, p. 459), arguments over which methodological approach is superior seem a bit off the mark. After all, proponents of quantitative methods have long acknowledged the fallibility and the value-laden context of scientific research (Lofland & Lofland, 1995). And for their part, qualitative researchers have searched for their own systems of quality control (i.e., trustworthiness).

Hanging over all of these points and counterpoints is a more pressing matter—the "crisis" facing social work research (Task Force on Social Work Research, 1991). According to a number of leading social work researchers (Fraser, 1994; Fraser & Taylor, 1990; Fraser, Taylor, Jackson, & O'Jack, 1991; Glisson, 1990; Task Force on Social Work Research, 1991), the main problem with the social work research literature is not epistemological but methodological—the lack of rigor. Although improving, social work journals still contain many studies with weak designs, unsupported conclusions, and inappropriate statistical tests (Fraser, 1994; Fraser et al., 1991). There is little reason to believe that qualitative studies are more rigorous than their quantitative counterparts.

Which brings us to the topic at hand: how to promote rigorous qualitative research in social work education. I will begin by discussing challenges at the individual level, move to the institutional level, and end with a few thoughts on qualitative methods and the research-practice conundrum in social work.

CHALLENGES AT THE
INDIVIDUAL LEVEL

If there is one thing that all qualitative researchers can agree on, it is this: Qualitative methods are not easy. Rewarding, even exhilarating, but never easy. We have already reviewed many of the challenges facing individuals who want to do qualitative research in a quantitative world, including commitments of time and energy (not to mention the ability to conceptualize and write). The absence of structured guidelines in qualitative methods is liberating, but also demanding (Wolcott, 1994). In short, qualitative research is not a good alternative for harried practitioners, doctoral students, or faculty seeking to avoid the regimentation of quantitative analyses.

For social work practitioners, there is another caveat: Qualitative methods do not fit well with a clinical mandate. As discussed in Chapter 1, it is virtually impossible for a clinician to carry out a rigorous qualitative study and simultaneously satisfy the clinical mandate with individual clients. It is better to design qualitative studies *of* practice than to attempt qualitative studies *in* practice. Beyond working with individual client systems, social work practice also embraces human services programs at the agency and community level. Here, qualitative methods are ideally suited to "black box" investigations. Whether devoted to general knowledge building or a target evaluation, qualitative approaches such as ethnography, focus group interviewing, and document analyses are uniquely valuable.

Academic settings generally offer a more favorable climate for the pursuit of qualitative research. Yet, a number of challenges confront social work faculty who wish to become qualitative researchers. Academic positions demand a lot—teaching, academic and field advisement, and seemingly endless committee meetings. These responsiblities leave limited time for any type of research, let alone qualitative research.

Then there are those pesky "dissemination problems" (Fraser et al., 1991, p. 26) that plague all qualitative researchers. Qualitative reports are invariably longer than the 25-page limit of most journals, and the lack of standardized criteria often hobbles peer review for the qualitative researcher (Drisko, 1997). To add insult to injury, academic publishers are not exactly falling over each other to publish book-length qualitative studies. For researchers in academia who need and want to publish their findings (for promotion and tenure as well as the more lofty goal of connecting with the scholarly world), qualitative research is not the quickest route to success.

Of course, all rigorous research takes painstaking effort and patience. No one embarks on a research career expecting a fast track to fame and fortune (Wolcott, 1994). In this context, it is all the more remarkable that so many social work researchers have embarked on their own journeys of discovery. Combining a thirst for knowledge with heavy doses of fortitude, these intellectual high achievers surmount the odds and do us proud.

CHALLENGES FOR
SCHOOLS OF SOCIAL WORK

Qualitative researchers in social work are a highly motivated bunch. Many are self-taught, others learned by taking courses in departments of sociology, anthropology, education, or nursing. In any event, institutional supports have lagged far behind individual effort.

Notwithstanding the endorsement of social work's national professional organizations, qualitative methods are almost invisible in the BSW and MSW curricula of schools of social work. Existing curricula at the baccalaureate and master's level are already so crowded that it is hard to justify adding new research courses to programs designed to train practitioners in 2 years or less.

Should we consider displacing quantitative methods in the BSW and MSW curricula? I am strongly opposed to such a move. Given the generally impoverished state of most schools' research cultures, more (not less) grounding in quantitative methods is needed by social work researchers to prepare them for a professional future in a world where accountability and measurable outcomes are necessary (and worthy) goals.

Doctoral programs would appear to be more fertile ground for qualitative methods because they afford a longer span of time for learning and doing qualitative research. Doctoral students are in a one-time only period in their lives when they can take several years to think about a topic of scholarly inquiry and pursue it to completion. For students entering doctoral education in the helping professions (social work, nursing, education, etc.), the attraction of qualitative methods can be powerful.

Yet, doctoral programs in social work have their own limitations in fostering a research culture. A study of the course content of the 47 active social work doctoral programs found neither the depth nor breadth of courses necessary to sustain rigorous research training (Fraser et al., 1991). The study's authors concluded that overextended faculty and fiscal resources prevented the kind of hands-on, skills-focused training widely acknowledged as the basis for research scholarship (Fraser et al., 1991). Compared to their counterparts in the social and behavioral sciences, doctoral students in social work are experienced professionals when they begin their studies. Many pursue doctoral studies part-time, juggling them with full-time jobs and family responsibilities. As well, many seek a doctorate for professional advancement and to pursue studies in advanced clinical practice rather than to enter full-time academic life. Given these tendencies, it is not surprising that so many doctoral students in social work cringe at the prospect of relearning (or learning for the first time) statistics and quantitative research designs.

Enter qualitative methods—a friendly, accessible approach that draws on the finely honed skills of interviewing that social work practitioners already possess. A match made in heaven? Yes, for those students ready and willing to take the plunge. But for many others, the allure of qualitative research fades quickly, and quantitative research emerges as a more expedient route to completing a dissertation. For such students, the "tried and true" nature of quantitative methods outweighs their disadvantages (Fortune, 1990).

The absence of a strong research culture in many schools of social work makes the qualitative alternative all the more challenging. Stretching overextended faculty resources and expanding curricula to accommodate new epistemologies and research methodologies is asking a lot, particularly of schools with impoverished research cultures. By contrast, the growing number of research-oriented schools are in better position to lead the way.

To take root in any school of social work, qualitative methods need infrastructure supports such as full-time faculty with qualitative expertise and a curriculum flexible enough to accommodate new disciplinary influences (and additional methods courses). Enhancing faculty expertise will take time, but it is an attainable goal. In the meantime, we can draw on our colleagues in sociology, anthropology, or education to teach the courses we need. (A welcome by-product of this type of outreach is the cross-fertilization of ideas that comes from collaboration with colleagues in other disciplines.)

Social work schools *train* in practice skills, but they also *educate* students to think independently and creatively. It is here that qualitative methods can make a valuable contribution. Deeply rooted in anthropology and sociology (with bits of philosophy, history, and the arts thrown in for good measure), qualitative methods open up new vistas for students by exposing them to the venerable traditions of ethnographic fieldwork, life histories, and in-depth case studies. Although the family of qualitative methods is so expansive that multiple courses are required to do it justice— courses in ethnography, historiography, case study analysis, and feminist theory just to name a few—even one course can help introduce students to the qualitative alternative.

The rapidly changing landscape of social work practice—and the dire budget cutbacks imposed on many social services agencies—can make learning about qualitative methods seem a less-than-urgent priority in preparing students for a professional future. Yet, the growth and sur- vival of the profession of social work depend on the development of a sound knowledge base, a base firmly grounded in empirical research. Knowledge building, in turn, depends on the degree of commitment to research reflected in the infrastructures of schools of social work (National Association of Deans and Directors of Schools of Social Work Task Force on Administrative Research Infrastructures Within Social Work Education Programs, 1997). Although crises in practice and policy are an ongoing concern in the profession, its capacity to survive (and thrive) depends on taking a longer view. In this context, qualitative methods can give added value to existing research curricula at both the master's and doctoral levels.

Assuming that a school of social work wishes to make the commitment to include qualitative methods, what else can be done? Practical supports are helpful, like purchasing qualitative analysis software and providing assistance for peer support groups. Reaching out to qualitative research colleagues in other schools (to teach courses, sit on dissertation commit- tees, and collaborate on research) brings an infusion of expertise and friendly support.

M.S.W. programs that encourage students to take more than two re- search courses have somewhat more room to maneuver. For example, an elective course on qualitative methods could be offered to students inter- ested in pursuing research careers. Even within the typical two-course sequence of required M.S.W. research courses, it still might be possible to incorporate a 3- to 6-week qualitative methods "module" into an advanced concentration research course.

In the most desirable scenario for a doctoral program, students would take two or more qualitative methods courses and draw on knowledgable faculty and peer support groups as they proceed through their preliminary examinations and dissertation research. Doctoral programs committed to working toward strengthening their research cultures can draw on assistance from their representative organization (GADE) and logistical supports from the IASWR and CSWE. GADE, for example, developed and disseminated model syllabi for research courses (including a course in qualitative methods) and published guidelines for quality in doctoral education (GADE, 1992). Most recently, CSWE is preparing model course outlines for publication and dissemination to instructors in schools of social work (Denise Burnette, personal communication, October 1997). The good news (from my vantage point) is that qualitative methods are an integral part of these efforts to strengthen social work research.

As we move toward stronger and more comprehensive research infrastructures in schools of social work, there are a few "role model" guidelines that we qualitative researchers can follow to help the process along (Ely et al., 1991):

- Be available to talk about qualitative methods (formally and informally) with colleagues and students.
- Support students who wish to pursue a career in qualitative research (they are very dedicated people who deserve all the support we can give them).
- Advocate for inclusion of qualitative methods (and exemplary qualitative studies) in the curriculum, in doctoral dissertations, and in speakers' forums for students and faculty.
- Collaborate in multimethod studies.
- Last (but most important of all!) do good qualitative research and disseminate your findings at conferences, seminars, and in print.

A LAST WORD ON QUALITATIVE METHODS AND THE PRACTICE-RESEARCH CONUNDRUM

There is a pressing need for social work researchers and practitioners to join together in a symbiotic quest for knowledge building. Throughout its history, the profession of social work has been ambivalent and uncertain about which methods are appropriate and desirable to advance the knowledge base of the profession (Fraser et al., 1991). It is tempting to say that social work research and practice are at a critical crossroads, but they have always been positioned at one juncture or another dating back to the Flexner report and the Scientific Charity Movement of the early 1900s (Dinerman & Geismar, 1984).

Qualitative approaches such as grounded theory have been described as having a "hand into glove" fit (Gilgun, 1994, p. 115) with social work practice. Yet, the transition from practitioner to qualitative researcher is not as smooth as it might appear to be (Padgett, in press). All empirical research, qualitative or quantitative, require a change from business as usual. Even the most unobtrusive approaches—public observation and analyses of existing data—make demands that tug us away from our usual roles.

When we examine clinical practice using a qualitative lens, new ways of understanding become possible. But we also face a challenge in empirical studies of practice—deciding what constitutes "research." If for no other reason, this issue needs to be addressed because it comes up in the context of human subjects protections. Institutional Review Boards at universities grapple with this regularly when reviewing applications from clinician researchers. Trying to decide where "usual practice" ends and qualitative research begins is made even more difficult when clinicians and researchers do not share the same terminology, definitions, or worldviews (Padgett, in press).

There is clearly a continuum of activities linked to practice, which— depending on one's standpoint—may or may not be considered research. Using the definition of a quantitative approach, research entails the systematic collection and statistical analysis of data according to a specified design. For most clinicians, this requires a degree of effort and expertise far removed from practice as usual. By comparison, qualitative methods appear to have a much lower threshold of entry—flexible designs, intensive interviewing, and no statistical analyses.

In Chapter 1 and elsewhere in this book, I argued that this seemingly low threshold of entry into qualitative methods is an illusion. Like their quantitative counterparts, qualitative methods are empirical, systematic, and expected to adhere to guidelines for rigor. Adherence may be weak or strong, but there is at least cognizance of the need for rigor.

Many social work researchers have crossed the threshold, applying an array of qualitative methods to studies of practice, including constructivist (Laird, 1994), naturalistic (Rodwell, 1987), narrative (Tobin, 1994), and discourse-analytic (Sherman, 1994) approaches. Far less common are full-scale qualitative studies replete with ethnographic observation and interviewing.

Qualitative methods are not a panacea, the long-sought cure for the practice-research gap. Indeed, single-system designs and rapid assessment measures are more amenable to evaluations of clinical practice than in-depth (and prolonged) observation and interviewing. Qualitative methods have much to recommend them, but their curative powers are limited.

There are no easy answers here, but we are better off knowing from the beginning what we are in for. Despite this caveat, I remain incurably optimistic that researchers and practitioners of good faith will find common ground in their pursuit of knowledge to advance the profession of social work.

Appendix A

COMPUTER SOFTWARE FOR
QUALITATIVE DATA ANALYSIS

SELECTED QUALITATIVE
SOFTWARE PROGRAMS AND
THEIR DEVELOPERS OR DISTRIBUTORS

ATLAS/ti: Scientific Software Development, c/o Thomas Muhr, Trautenaustr. 12, 10717 Berlin, Germany. Telephone: +49-30-861-1415. Fax: +40 30 86 42 03 80. E-mail: sales@atlasti.de. World Wide Web: http://www.atlasti.de

HyperQUAL: Raymond V. Padilla, 3327 N. Dakota, Chandler, AZ 85224. Telephone: (602)892-9173. E-mail: iacrvp@asuvm.inre.asu.edu

HyperRESEARCH: Researchware, Inc., P.O. Box 1258, Randolph, MA 02368-1258. Telephone: (617)961-3909. E-mail: researchwr@aol.com

NUD•IST: In the United States and Canada: Scolari c/o Sage Publications Software, 2455 Teller Road, Thousand Oaks, CA 91320. Telephone: (805)499-1325. FAX: (805)499-0871. E-mail: nudist@sagepub.com. World Wide Web: http://www.sagepub.com. In Australia and New Zealand: Lorraine Davies, e-mail: lorraine@qsr.com.au

QUALPRO: Impulse Development Co., 3491-11 Thomasville Rd., Suite 202, Tallahassee, FL 32308. Telephone: (904)668-9865. Fax: (904)668-9866.

The Ethnograph: Qualis Research Associates, P.O. Box 2070, Amherst, MA 01004. Telephone: (413)256-8835. Fax: (413)256-8472. E-mail: qualis@qualisresearch.com. World Wide Web: http://www.qualisresearch.com

FURTHER READINGS
ON COMPUTER SOFTWARE
IN QUALITATIVE RESEARCH

Fielding, N. G., & Lee, R. M. (Eds.). (1991). *Using computers in qualitative research.* London: Sage.

Hesse-Biber, S., Dupuis, P., & Kinder, T. S. (1991). HyperRESEARCH: A computer program for the analysis of qualitative data with an emphasis on hypothesis testing and multimedia analysis. *Qualitative Sociology, 14,* 289-306.

Miles, M. B., & Weitzman, E. A. (1994). Choosing computer programs for qualitative data analysis. In M. B. Miles & A. M. Huberman (Eds.), *Qualitative data analysis: An expanded sourcebook* (2nd ed., pp. 311-317). Thousand Oaks, CA: Sage.

Muhr, T. (1991). ATLAS/ti: A prototype for the support of text interpretation. *Qualitative Sociology, 14,* 349-371.

Pfaffenberger, B. (1988). *Microcomputer applications in qualitative research.* Newbury Park, CA: Sage.

Richards, T. J., & Richards, L. (1994). Using computers in qualitative research. In N .K. Denzin & Y. S. Lincoln (Eds.), *Handbook of qualitative research* (pp. 445-462). Thousand Oaks, CA: Sage.

Seidel, J. V., & Clark, J. A. (1984). The Ethnograph: A computer program for the analysis of qualitative data. *Qualitative Sociology, 7,* 110-125.

Tesch, R. (1990). *Qualitative research: Analysis types and software tools.* New York: Falmer.

Tesch, R. (Ed.). (1991). Computers and qualitative data. *Qualitative Sociology, 13*(3 & 4) [Special issues, Parts 1 and 2].

Weitzman, E. A., & Miles, M. B. (1994). *Computer programs for qualitative data analysis.* Thousand Oaks, CA: Sage.

Appendix B

GUIDELINES FOR WRITING A QUALITATIVE RESEARCH PROPOSAL

Qualitative research proposals are no different from quantitative research proposals when it comes to two critical needs: (a) the need to present a tightly reasoned argument for why the research is important; and (b) the need to provide a description of the procedures to be employed and strategies for rigor. The suggested outline that follows resembles a quantitative research proposal in every respect except one: Qualitative proposals contain descriptions of qualitative methods in general (their epistemological origins and alternative modes of operation) and specifically (the particular method chosen for the proposed study). Although this additional information may be unnecessary in the future, it is wise to inform faculty and grant reviewers about qualitative methods and how they can be successfully applied.

The following is a suggested list of the basic components of a qualitative proposal:

1. Title page
2. Budget (including personnel, equipment, software, supplies, transportation costs, etc.)
3. Budget justification (explains roles of research personnel, rationale for equipment, software, incentive payments to respondents, transportation costs, transcription costs, etc.)
4. Specific aims/abstract (an overview of the study's goals)

5. Introduction/background to the study (an introduction to the topic, review of the literature, and overarching rationale for the study)
6. Methodology of the study
   a. Introduction to qualitative methods
   b. Introduction of specific methodology and approach (grounded theory, narrative analysis, case study, etc.)
   c. Description of setting (field site) and proposed respondents
   d. Sampling strategies
   e. Data sources and data collection procedures
   f. Data management and analysis procedures
   g. Strategies for rigor

7. Timetable for completing the study
8. Human participants protections (including informed consent, confidentiality, inclusion of women and minorities, etc.)
9. References

Research proposals may also include (in appendices):

- A summary of the pilot study results
- Biographical sketches (or full curriculum vitae) of the key participants
- Letters of approval from cooperating institutions
- Copies of the interview protocol (including consent forms)
- Any publications by the researcher related to the topic being studied

As described in Chapter 10, proposals for multimethod studies would be expanded and adjusted as necessary to accommodate both methods. For more detailed advice about how to write a qualitative research proposal, see Morse (1994) and Munhall (1994).

REFERENCES

Agar, M. H. (1980). *The professional stranger: An informal introduction to ethnography.* New York: Academic Press.

Agar, M. H. (1991). The right brain strikes back. In N. G. Fielding & R. M. Lee (Eds.), *Using computers in qualitative research* (pp. 181-194). Newbury Park, CA: Sage.

Akeroyd, A. V. (1991). Personal information and qualitative research data: Some practical and ethical problems arising from data protection legislation. In N. G. Fielding & R. M. Lee (Eds.), *Using computers in qualitative research* (pp. 88-106). Newbury Park, CA: Sage.

Allen-Meares, P. (1995). Applications of qualitative research: Let the work begin. *Social Work Research, 19,* 5-8.

Altheide, D. L., & Johnson, J. M. (1994). Criteria for assessing interpretive validity in qualitative research. In N. K. Denzin & Y. S. Lincoln (Eds.), *Handbook of qualitative research* (pp. 485-499). Thousand Oaks, CA: Sage.

Atkinson, P. (1990). *The ethnographic imagination: Textual constructions of reality.* London: Routledge.

Atkinson, P., & Hammersley, M. (1994). Ethnography and participant observation. In N. K. Denzin & Y. S. Lincoln (Eds.), *Handbook of qualitative research* (pp. 236-247). Thousand Oaks, CA: Sage.

Becker, H., Geer, B., Hughes, E., & Strauss, A. (1961). *Boys in white: Student culture in medical school.* Chicago: University of Chicago Press.

Beeman, S. (1995). Maximizing credibility and accountability in qualitative data collection and data analysis: A social work research case example. *Journal of Sociology and Social Welfare, 22,* 99-114.

Berelson, B. (1952). *Content analysis in communication research.* Glencoe, IL: Free Press.

Berlin, S. (1990). Dichotomous and complex thinking. *Social Service Review, 64,* 46-59.

Bernstein, S. T., & Epstein, I. (1994). Grounded theory meets the reflective practitioner: Integrating qualitative and quantitative methods in administrative practice.

In E. Sherman & W. J. Reid (Eds.), *Qualitative research in social work* (pp. 435-444). New York: Columbia University Press.

Blake, R. L. (1989). Integrating quantitative and qualitative methods in family research. *Family Systems Medicine, 7,* 411-427.

Blakely, C. H., Mayer, J. P., Gotterhalk, R. G., Schmitt, N., Davidson, W. S., Roitman, D. B., & Emshoff, J. G. (1987). The fidelity-adaptation debate: Implications for the implementation of public sector social programs. *American Journal of Community Psychology, 15,* 253-268.

Bogdan, R. C., & Taylor, S. J. (1975). *Introduction to qualitative research.* New York: John Wiley.

Bogdan, R. C., & Taylor, S. J. (1994). A positive approach to qualitative evaluation and policy research in social work. In E. Sherman & W. J. Reid (Eds.), *Qualitative research in social work* (pp. 293-302). New York: Columbia University Press.

Bosk, C. L. (1979). *Forgive and remember: Managing medical failure.* Chicago: University of Chicago Press.

Brewer, J., & Hunter, A. (1989). *Multimethod research: A synthesis of styles.* Newbury Park, CA: Sage

Bruner, J. (1987). Life as narrative. *Social Research, 54,* 11-32.

Bryman, A. (1988). *Quantity and quality in social research.* London: Unwin Hyman.

Burnette, D. (1994). Managing chronic illness alone in late life: Sisyphus at work. In C. K. Riessman (Ed.), *Qualitative studies in social work research* (pp. 5-27). Thousand Oaks, CA: Sage.

Burns, B. J., & Santos, A. B. (1995). Assertive community treatment: An update of randomized trials. *Psychiatric Services, 46,* 669-675.

Campbell, D. T., & Stanley, J. C. (1963). *Experimental and quasi-experimental designs for research.* Boston: Houghton-Mifflin.

Cancian, F. M. (1993). Conflicts between activist research and academic success: Participatory research and alternative strategies. *The American Sociologist, 81,* 92-106.

Carling, P. J. (1993). Housing and supports for persons with mental illness: Emerging approaches to research and practice. *Hospital and Community Psychiatry, 44,* 439-449.

Chambon, A., & Irving, A. (1994). *Essays on postmodernism in social work.* Toronto: Canadian Scholars' Press.

Clifford, J., & Marcus, G. E. (Eds.). (1986). *Writing culture: The poetics and politics of ethnography.* Berkeley: University of California Press.

Cohler, B. J. (1994). The human sciences, the life story, and clinical research. In E. Sherman & W. J. Reid (Eds.), *Qualitative research in social work* (pp. 163-174). New York: Columbia University Press.

Combs-Orme, T. (1990). The interface of qualitative and quantitative methods in social work research. In L. Videka-Sherman & W. J. Reid (Eds.), *Advances in clinical social work research* (pp. 181-188). Washington, DC: NASW Press.

Cook, T. D., & Campbell, D. T. (1979). *Quasi-experimentation: Design and analysis issues for field settings.* Boston: Houghton-Mifflin.

Cook, T. D., & Reichardt, C. S. (Eds.). (1979). *Qualitative and quantitative methods in evaluation research.* Beverly Hills, CA: Sage.

Creswell, J. W. (1994). *Research design: Qualitative and quantitative approaches.* Thousand Oaks, CA: Sage.

Daniels, A. K. (1983). Self-deception and self-discovery in fieldwork. *Qualitative Sociology, 6,* 195-214.

Davis, I. (1994). Integrating qualitative and quantitative methods in clinical research. In E. Sherman & W. J. Reid (Eds.), *Qualitative research in social work* (pp. 423-434). New York: Columbia University Press.

Davis, L. V. (1994). Is feminist research inherently qualitative, or is it a fundamentally different approach? In W. W. Hudson & P. S. Nurius (Eds.), *Controversial issues in social work research* (pp. 63-74). Boston: Allyn & Bacon.

Dehar, M., Casswell, S., & Duignan, P. (1993). Formative and process evaluation of health promotion and disease prevention programs. *Evaluation Review, 17,* 204-220.

Denzin, N. K. (1978). *The research act: A theoretical introduction to sociological methods* (2nd ed.). New York: McGraw-Hill.

Denzin, N. K. (1994). The art and politics of interpretation. In N. K. Denzin & Y. S. Lincoln (Eds.), *Handbook of qualitative research* (pp. 500-515). Thousand Oaks, CA: Sage.

Denzin, N. K., & Lincoln, Y. S. (Eds.). (1994). *Handbook of qualitative research.* Thousand Oaks, CA: Sage.

Dinerman, M., & Geismar, L. L. (Eds.). (1984). *A quarter-century of social work education.* New York: National Association of Social Workers and Council on Social Work Education.

Donmoyer, R. (1990). Generalizability and the single-case study. In E. W. Eisner & A. Peshkin (Eds.), *Qualitative inquiry in education: The continuing debate* (pp. 175-200). New York: Teachers College Press.

Drake, R. E., Bebout, R. R., Quimby, E., Teague, G. B., Harris, M., & Roach, J. P. (1993). Process evaluation in the Washington D.C. Dual Diagnosis Project. *Alcoholism Treatment Quarterly, 10,* 113-124.

Drisko, J. W. (1997). Strengthening qualitative studies and reports: Standards to promote academic integrity. *Journal of Social Work Education, 33,* 185-197.

Edelson, M. (1994). Can psychotherapy research answer this psychotherapist's questions? In P. F. Talley, H. H. Strupp, & S. F. Butler (Eds.), *Psychotherapy research and practice* (pp. 60-87). New York: Basic Books.

Elkin, I., Shea, M. T., Watkins, J. T., Imber, S. D., Lotsky, S. M., Collins, J. F., Glass, D. R., Pilkonis, P. A., Weber, W. R., Docherty, J. P., Fiester, S. J., & Parloff, M. B. (1989). NIMH treatment of depression collaborative research program: General effectiveness of treatments. *Archives of General Psychiatry, 46,* 971-983.

Ellis, C., & Flaherty, M. G. (1992). An agenda for the interpretation of lived experience. In E. Ellis & M. G. Flaherty (Eds.), *Investigating subjectivity: Research on lived experience* (pp. 1-16). Newbury Park, CA: Sage.

Ely, M. (with Anzul, M., Friedman, T., Garner, D., & Steinmetz, A. M.). (1991). *Doing qualitative research: Circles within circles.* London: Falmer.

Emerson, R. M., Fretz, R. I., & Shaw, L. L. (1995). *Writing ethnographic fieldnotes.* Chicago: University of Chicago Press.

England, S. E. (1994). Modeling theory from fiction and autobiography. In C. K. Riessman (Ed.), *Qualitative studies in social work research* (pp. 190-213). Thousand Oaks, CA: Sage.

Estroff, S. (1981). *Making it crazy.* Berkeley: University of California Press.

Everett, B., & Boydell, K. (1994). A methodology for including consumers' opinions in mental health evaluation research. *Hospital and Community Psychiatry, 45,* 76-78.

Fals-Borda, O., & Rahman, M. A. (Eds.). (1991). *Action and knowledge: Breaking the monopoly with participatory action research.* New York: Intermediate Technology/Apex.

Feagin, J. R., Orum, A. M., & Sjoberg, G. (Eds.). (1991). *A case for the case study.* Chapel Hill: University of North Carolina Press.

Fetterman, D. M. (1989). *Ethnography step by step.* Newbury Park, CA: Sage.

Fielding, N. G., & Lee, R. M. (Eds.). (1991). *Using computers in qualitative research.* London: Sage.

Firestone, W. A. (1990). Accommodation. Toward a paradigm-praxis dialectic. In E. G. Guba (Ed.), *The paradigm dialog* (pp. 105-124). Newbury Park, CA: Sage.

Fischer, J. (1973). Has mighty casework struck out? *Social Work, 18,* 5-20.

Fonow, M. M., & Cook, J. A. (Eds.). (1991). *Beyond methodology: Feminist scholarship as lived research.* Bloomington: Indiana University Press.

Fontana, A., & Frey, J. H. (1994). Interviewing: The art of science. In N. K. Denzin & Y. S. Lincoln (Eds.), *Handbook of qualitative research* (pp. 361-376). Thousand Oaks, CA: Sage.

Fortune, A. E. (1990). Synthesis: Problems and uses of qualitative methodologies. In L. Videka-Sherman & W. J. Reid (Eds.), *Advances in clinical social work research* (pp. 194-201). Washington, DC: NASW Press.

Fraser, M., & Haapala, D. (1987). Home-based family treatment: A quantitative-qualitative assessment. *The Journal of Applied Sciences, 12,* 1-23.

Fraser, M. W. (1994). Scholarship and research in social work: Emerging challenges. *Journal of Social Work Education, 30,* 252-266.

Fraser, M. W., & Taylor, M. J. (1990). *An assessment of the literature in social work: Final report to the NIMH Task Force on Social Work Research.* Salt Lake City: University of Utah, School of Social Work, Social Research Institute.

Fraser, M. W., Taylor, M. J., Jackson, R., & O'Jack, J. (1991). Social work and science: Many ways of knowing? *Social Work Research & Abstracts, 17,* 5-15.

Friedman, T. (1991). Feeling. In M. Ely (with M. Anzul, T. Friedman, D. Garner, & A. M. Steinmetz), *Doing qualitative research: Circles within circles* (pp. 107-138). London: Falmer.

Gambrill, E. (1995). Less marketing and more scholarship. *Social Work Research, 19,* 38-48.

Gambrill, E. D. (1990). *Critical thinking in social work practice: Improving the accuracy of judgments and decisions about clients.* San Francisco: Jossey-Bass.

Garner, D. (1991). Interpreting. In M. Ely (with M. Anzul, T. Friedman, D. Garner, & A. M. Steinmetz), *Doing qualitative research: Circles within circles* (pp. 139-178). London: Falmer.

Geertz, C. (1973). *The interpretation of cultures: Selected essays.* New York: Basic Books.

Geertz, C. (1983). *Local knowledge: Further essays in interpretive anthropology.* New York: Basic Books.

Geertz, C. (1988). *Works and lives: The anthropologist as author.* Stanford, CA: Stanford University Press.

Gergen, K. J. (1985). The social constructionist movement in modern psychology. *The American Psychologist, 40,* 266-275.

Gilgun, J. F. (1994). Hand into glove: The grounded theory approach and social work practice research. In E. Sherman & W. J. Reid (Eds.), *Qualitative research in social work* (pp. 115-125). New York: Columbia University Press.

Glaser, B. (1992). *Basics of ground theory analysis.* Mill Valley, CA: Sociology Press.

Glaser, B. G. (1978). *Theoretical sensitivity.* Mill Valley, CA: Sociology Press.

Glaser, B. G., & Strauss, A. L. (1967). *The discovery of grounded theory: Strategies for qualitative research.* Chicago: Aldine.

Glisson, C. (1990). *A systematic assessment of the social work literature: Trends in social work research.* Knoxville: University of Tennessee, College of Social Work.

Goetz, J., & LeCompte, M. (1984). *Ethnography and qualitative design in educational research.* Orlando, FL: Academic Press.

Goffman, E. (1959). *The presentation of self in everyday life.* Garden City, NY: Basic Books.

Goffman, E. (1961). *Asylums: Essays on the social situation of mental patients and other inmates.* Garden City, NY: Basic Books.

Goisman, R. M. (1997). Cognitive-behavioral therapy today. *Harvard Mental Health Letter, 13,* 4-7.

Goldstein, H. (1981). Qualitative research and social work practice: Partners in discovery. *Journal of Sociology and Social Welfare, 18,* 101-121.

Greenbaum, T. L. (1993). *The handbook for focus group research.* New York: Lexington Books.

Greene, J. C. (1994). Qualitative program evaluation: Practice and promise. In N. K. Denzin & Y. S. Lincoln (Eds.), *Handbook of qualitative research* (pp. 530-544). Thousand Oaks, CA: Sage.

Grigsby, R. K. (1992). Mental health consultation at a youth shelter: An ethnographic approach. *Child & Youth Care Forum 21,* 249-261.

Grinnell, R. M., Jr. (1997). *Social work research and evaluation: Quantitative and qualitative approaches.* Itasca, IL: F. E. Peacock.

Group for the Advancement of Doctoral Education (GADE). (1992). *Guidelines for quality in social work doctoral programs.* Washington, DC: National Institute of Mental Health.

Guba, E. G. (Ed.). (1990). *The paradigm dialog.* Newbury Park, CA: Sage.

Guba, E. G., & Lincoln, Y. S. (1981). *Effective evaluation.* San Francisco: Jossey-Bass.

Guba, E. G., & Lincoln, Y. S. (1989). *Fourth generation evaluation*. Newbury Park, CA: Sage.

Guba, E. G., & Lincoln, Y. S. (1994). Competing paradigms in qualitative research. In N. K. Denzin & Y. S. Lincoln (Eds.), *Handbook of qualitative research* (pp. 105-117). Thousand Oaks, CA: Sage.

Haase, J. E., & Myers, S. T. (1988). Reconciling paradigm assumptions of qualitative and quantitative research. *Western Journal of Nursing Research, 10,* 128-137.

Hammersley, M. (1992). *What's wrong with ethnography? Methodological explorations.* London: Routledge.

Harding, S. (1986). *The science question in feminism.* Ithaca, NY: Cornell University Press.

Harris, M. (1968). *The rise of anthropological theory.* New York: Columbia University Press.

Harrison, W. D. (1994). The inevitability of integrated methods. In E. Sherman & W. J. Reid (Eds.), *Qualitative research in social work* (pp. 409-422). New York: Columbia University Press.

Hartman, A. (1994). Setting the theme: Many ways of knowing. In E. Sherman & W. J. Reid (Eds.), *Qualitative research in social work* (pp. 459-463). New York: Columbia University Press.

Hatfield, A. (1993). A family perspective on supported housing. *Hospital and Community Psychiatry, 44,* 496-497.

Heineman-Pieper, M. (1981). The obsolete scientific imperative in social work research. *Social Service Review, 55,* 371-396.

Hertz, R., & Imber, J. B. (Eds.). (1995). *Studying elites using qualitative methods.* Thousand Oaks, CA: Sage.

Hochschild, A. (1983). *The managed heart: Commercialization of human feeling.* Berkeley: University of California Press.

Hochschild, A. (with Machung, A.). (1989). *The second shift: Inside the two-job marriage.* New York: Avon.

Hogarty, G. E., Anderson, C. M., Reiss, D. J., Kornblith, S. J., Greenwald, D. P. Javna, C. D., & Madonia, M. J. (1986). Family psychoeducation, social skills training, and maintenance chemotherapy in the aftercare treatment of schizophrenia. *Archives of General Psychiatry, 43,* 633-642.

Holstein, J. A., & Gubrium, J. F. (1994). Phenomenology, ethnomethodology, and interpretive practice. In N. K. Denzin & Y. S. Lincoln (Eds.), *Handbook of qualitative research* (pp. 262-272). Thousand Oaks, CA: Sage.

House, E. R. (1980). *Evaluating with validity.* Beverly Hills, CA: Sage.

Howe, K. (1988). Against the qualitative-quantitative incompatibility: A diagnosis diehard. *Educational Researcher, 17,* 10-16.

Huberman, A. M., & Miles, M. B. (1994). Data management and analysis methods. In N. K. Denzin & Y. S. Lincoln (Eds.), *Handbook of qualitative research* (pp. 428-444). Thousand Oaks, CA: Sage.

Hudson, W. W., & Nurius, P. S. (1994). *Controversial issues in social work research.* Boston: Allyn and Bacon.

Humphries, L. (1970). *Tearoom trade: Impersonal sex in public places.* Chicago: Aldine.

Hyde, C. (1994). Reflections on a journey: A research story. In C. K. Riessman (Ed.), *Qualitative studies in social work research* (pp. 169-189). Thousand Oaks, CA: Sage.

Imre, R. W. (1990). Commentary: Epistemological and semantic traps. In L. Videka-Sherman & W. J. Reid (Eds.), *Advances in clinical social work research* (pp. 366-370). Washington, DC: NASW Press.

Inui, T. S., & Frankel, R. M. (1991). Evaluating the quality of qualitative research. *Journal of General Internal Medicine, 6,* 485-487.

Janesick, V. J. (1994). The dance of qualitative research design: Metaphor, methodolatry, and meaning. In N. K. Denzin & Y. S. Lincoln (Eds.), *Handbook of qualitative research* (pp. 209-219). Thousand Oaks, CA: Sage.

Jick, T. (1983). Mixing qualitative and quantitative methods: Triangulation in action. In J. Van Maanen (Ed.), *Qualitative Methodology* (pp. 135-148). Beverly Hills: Sage.

Kasper, A. S. (1994). A feminist, qualitative methodology: A study of women with breast cancer. *Qualitative Sociology, 17,* 263-281.

Kirk, J., & Miller, M. L. (1986). *Reliability and validity in qualitative research.* Newbury Park, CA: Sage.

Krueger, R. A. (1994). *Focus groups: A practical guide for applied research* (2nd ed.). Thousand Oaks, CA: Sage.

Kübler-Ross, E. (1969). *On death and dying.* New York: Macmillan.

Kuhn, T. (1970). *The structure of scientific revolutions.* Chicago: University of Chicago Press.

Labov, W., & Waletzky, J. (1967). Narrative analysis: Oral versions of personal experience. In J. Helm (Ed.), *Essays on the verbal and visual arts* (pp. 12-44). Seattle: University of Washington Press.

Laird, J. (1994). "Thick description" re-visited: Family therapist as anthropologist-constructivist. In E. Sherman & W. J. Reid (Eds.), *Qualitative research in social work* (pp. 175-189). New York: Columbia University Press.

Lamb, H., & Lamb, D. (1990). Factors contributing to homelessness among the chronically and severely mentally ill. *Hospital and Community Psychiatry, 41,* 301-305.

Langellier, K. M. (1989). Personal narratives: Perspectives on theory and research. *Text and Performance Quarterly, 9,* 243-276.

LaPiere, R. T. (1934). Attitudes vs. actions. *Social Forces, 13,* 230-237.

Lévi-Strauss, C. (1966). *The savage mind* (2nd ed.). Chicago: University of Chicago Press.

Levine, I. S., & Zimmerman, J. D. (1996). Using qualitative data to inform public policy: Evaluating "Choose to De-Fuse." *American Journal of Orthopsychiatry, 66,* 363-377.

Liebow, E. (1967). *Talley's Corner: A study of Negro street corner men.* Boston: Little, Brown.

Liebow, E. (1993). *Tell them who I am: The lives of homeless women.* New York: Penguin.

Lincoln, Y. S., & Guba, E. G. (1985). *Naturalistic inquiry.* Beverly Hills, CA: Sage.

Linehan, M. M., Armstrong, H. E., Suarez, A., Allmon, D., & Heard, H. L. (1991). Behavioral treatment of chronically parasuicidal borderline patients. *Archives of General Psychiatry, 48,* 1060-1064.

Lipman-Blumen, J. (1987). *Individual and organizational achieving styles: A handbook for researchers and human resource professionals.* Claremont, CA: Achieving Styles Institute.

Lofland, J., & Lofland, L. (1995). *Analyzing social settings: A guide to qualitative observation and analysis* (3rd ed.). Belmont, CA: Wadsworth.

Lu, Y. E. (1994). A comparison of achieving styles of Asian American and non-Asian American psychotherapists. *Psychotherapy in Private Practice, 13,* 45-69.

Lu, Y. E. (1996). Underutilization of mental health services by Asian American clients: The impact of language and culture in clinical assessment and intervention. *Psychotherapy in Private Practice, 15,* 43-59.

Lynd, R. S., & Lynd, H. M. (1937). *Middletown in transition: A study in cultural conflicts.* New York: Harcourt Brace.

Lynd, R. S., & Lynd, H. M. (1956). *Middletown: A study in modern American culture.* New York: Harcourt Brace.

MacGregor, P. (1994). Grief: The unrecognized parental response to mental illness in a child. *Social Work, 39,* 160-166.

Maling, M. S., & Howard, K. I. (1994). From research to practice to research to . . . In P. F. Talley, H. H. Strupp, & S. F. Butler (Eds.), *Psychotherapy research and practice* (pp. 246-253). New York: Basic Books.

Malinowski, B. (1967). *A diary in the strict sense of the term.* New York: Harcourt Brace.

Manicas, P. T., & Secord, P. F. (1982). Implications for psychology of the new philosophy of science. *American Psychologist, 38,* 390-413.

Manwar, A., Johnson, B. D., & Dunlap, E. (1994). Qualitative data analysis with Hypertext: A case of New York City crack dealers. *Qualitative Sociology, 17,* 283-292.

Marcus, G. E. (1994). What comes (just) after "post"? The case of ethnography. In N. K. Denzin & Y. S. Lincoln (Eds.), *Handbook of qualitative research* (pp. 563-574). Thousand Oaks, CA: Sage.

Mariano, C. (1990). Qualitative research: Instructional strategies and curricular considerations. *Nursing and Health Care, 11,* 354-359.

Marshall, C. (1990). Goodness criteria: Are they objective or judgment calls? In E. G. Guba (Ed.), *The paradigm dialog* (pp. 188-197). Newbury Park, CA: Sage.

Marshall, C., & Rossman, G. B. (1995). *Designing qualitative research* (2nd ed.). Thousand Oaks, CA: Sage.

Mathews, H., Lannin, D. R., & Mitchell, J. P. (1992). Coming to terms with advanced breast cancer: Black women's narratives from eastern North Carolina. *Social Science and Medicine, 38,* 789-800.

Mathison, S. (1988). Why triangulate? *Educational Researcher, 17,* 13-17.

McCracken, G. (1988). *The long interview.* Newbury Park, CA: Sage.

McFarlane, W. R., Link, B., Dushay, R., Marchal, J., & Crilly, J. (1994). Psychoeducational multiple family groups: Four-year relapse outcome in schizophrenia. *Family Process, 34,* 127-144.

Merton, R. K., Fiske, M., & Kendall, P. (1956). *The focused interview.* Glencoe, IL: Free Press.

Meyer, C. H. (1990). Commentary: The forest or the trees? In L. Videka-Sherman & W. J. Reid (Eds.), *Advances in clinical social work research* (pp. 395-399). Washington, DC: NASW Press.

Miles, M. B., & Huberman, A. M. (Eds.). (1994). *Qualitative data analysis: An expanded sourcebook* (2nd ed.). Thousand Oaks, CA: Sage.

Miles, M. B., & Weitzman, E. A. (1994). Choosing computer programs for qualitative data analysis. In M. B. Miles & A. M. Huberman (Eds.), *Qualitative data analysis: An expanded sourcebook* (2nd ed.). Thousand Oaks, CA: Sage.

Milgram, S. (1963). Behavioral study of obedience. *Journal of Abnormal and Social Psychology, 67,* 371-378.

Mishler, E. (1986). *Research interviewing: Context and narrative.* Cambridge, MA: Harvard University Press.

Mizrahi, T., & Abramson, J. S. (1994). Collaboration between social workers and physicians: An emerging typology. In E. Sherman & W. J. Reid (Eds.), *Qualitative research in social work* (pp. 135-151). New York: Columbia University Press.

Morgan, D. L. (1988). *Focus groups as qualitative research.* Newbury Park, CA: Sage.

Morse, J. M. (1991). Approaches to qualitative-quantitative methodological triangulation. *Nursing Research, 40,* 120-123.

Morse, J. M. (1994). Designing funded qualitative research. In N. K. Denzin & Y. S. Lincoln (Eds.), *Handbook of qualitative research* (pp. 220-235). Thousand Oaks, CA: Sage.

Munhall, P. L. (1994). *Qualitative research proposals and reports: A guide.* New York: National League for Nursing Press.

Myerhoff, B. (1978). Number our days: A triumph of continuity and culture among Jewish old people in an urban ghetto. New York: Simon & Schuster.

Myers, L. L., & Thyer, B. A. (1997). Should social work clients have the right to effective treatment? *Social Work, 42,* 288-298.

National Association of Deans and Directors of Schools of Social Work Task Force on Administrative Research Infrastructures Within Social Work Education Programs. (1997). *Challenges and opportunities for promoting federally funded research in social work programs.* Washington, DC: Institute for the Advancement of Social Work Research.

Noblit, G. W. (1988, February). *A sense of interpretation.* Paper presented at the Ethnography in Education Research Forum, Philadelphia.

Oakley, A. (1981). Interviewing women: A contradiction in terms. In H. Roberts (Ed.), *Doing feminist research* (pp. 30-61). London: Routledge & Kegan Paul.

Orlinsky, D. E. (1994). Research-based knowledge as the emergent foundation for clinical practice in psychotherapy. In P. F. Talley, H. H. Strupp, & S. F. Butler (Eds.), *Psychotherapy research and practice* (pp. 99-123). New York: Basic Books.

Padgett, D. K. (in press). Does the glove really fit? Qualitative research and clinical social work practice. *Social Work.*

Padgett, D. K., Patrick, C., Burns, B. J., & Schlesinger, H. S. (1994). Ethnicity and use of outpatient mental health services in a national insured population. *American Journal of Public Health, 84,* 222-226.

Padgett, D. K., Yedidia, M., Kerner, J., & Mandelblatt, J. (1996, September). *Barriers to follow-up of an abnormal mammogram among African-American women: Preliminary qualitative findings from the NYU-Georgetown Mammogram Study.* Paper presented at the National Conference on Women's Health, Washington, DC.

Painter, N. I. (1979). *The narrative of Hosea Hudson: His life as a Negro communist in the South.* Cambridge, MA: Harvard University Press.

Patton, M. Q. (1986). *Utilization-focused evaluation* (2nd ed.). Beverly Hills, CA: Sage.

Patton, M. Q. (1990). *Qualitative evaluation and research methods* (2nd ed.). Newbury Park, CA: Sage.

Pieper, M. H. (1989). The heuristic paradigm: A unifying and comprehensive approach to social work research. *Smith College Studies in Social Work, 60,* 8-34.

Polkinghorne, D. E. (1988). *Narrative knowing and the human sciences.* Albany: State University of New York Press.

Powdermaker, H. (1966). *Stranger and friend: The way of an anthropologist.* New York: W. W. Norton.

Proctor, E. (1990). Evaluating clinical practice: Issues of purpose and design. *Social Work Research and Abstracts, 26,* 32-40.

Pulice, R. T. (1994). Qualitative evaluation methods in the public sector: Understanding and working with constituency groups in the evaluation process. In W. Sherman & W. J. Reid (Eds.), *Qualitative research in social work* (pp. 303-314). New York: Columbia University Press.

Pulice, R. T., McCormick, L. L., & Dewees, M. (1995). A qualitative approach to assessing the effects of system change on consumers, families, and providers. *Psychiatric Services, 46,* 575-579.

Punch, M. (1994). Politics and ethics in qualitative research. In N. K. Denzin & Y. S. Lincoln (Eds.), *Handbook of qualitative research* (pp. 83-97). Thousand Oaks, CA: Sage.

Rabinow, P., & Sullivan, W. M. (Eds.). (1979). *Interpretive social science: A reader.* Berkeley: University of California Press.

Reason, P. (1994). Three approaches to participative inquiry. In N. K. Denzin & Y. S. Lincoln (Eds.), *Handbook of qualitative research* (pp. 324-339). Thousand Oaks, CA: Sage.

Reid, W. J. (1994). The empirical practice movement. *Social Service Review, 68,* 165-184.

Reinharz, R. (1992). *Feminist methods in social research.* New York: Oxford University Press.

Richards, T. J., & Richards, L. (1994). Using computers in qualitative research. In N. K. Denzin & Y. S. Lincoln (Eds.), *Handbook of qualitative research* (pp. 445-462). Thousand Oaks, CA: Sage.

Richardson, L. (1990). *Writing strategies.* Newbury Park, CA: Sage.

Richardson, L. (1994). Writing: A method of inquiry. In N. K. Denzin & Y. S. Lincoln (Eds.), *Handbook of qualitative research* (pp. 516-529). Thousand Oaks, CA: Sage.

Ridgway, P., & Zipple, A. M. (1990). The paradigm shift in residential services: From the linear continuum to supported housing approaches. *Psychosocial Rehabilitation Journal, 13,* 20-31.

Riessman, C. K. (1990). *Divorce talk: Women and men make sense of personal relationships.* Rutgers, NJ: Rutgers University Press.

Riessman, C. K. (1993). *Narrative analysis.* Newbury Park, CA: Sage.

Riessman, C. K. (Ed.). (1994). *Qualitative studies in social work research.* Thousand Oaks, CA: Sage.

Rodwell, M. K. (1987). Naturalistic inquiry: An alternative model for social work assessment. *Social Service Review, 61,* 231-246.

Rodwell, M. K., & Woody, D. (1994). Constructivist evaluation: The policy/practice context. In E. Sherman & W. J. Reid (Eds.), *Qualitative research in social work* (pp. 315-327). New York: Columbia University Press.

Rosaldo, R. (1989). *Culture and truth: The remaking of social analysis.* Boston: Beacon.

Ruckdeschel, R., Earnshaw, P., & Firrek, A. (1994). The qualitative case study and evaluation: Issues, methods, and examples. In E. Sherman & W. J. Reid (Eds.), *Qualitative research in social work* (pp. 251-264). New York: Columbia University Press.

Saleeby, D. (1989). The estrangement of knowing and doing: Professions in crisis. *Social Casework, 70,* 556-563.

Salomon, G. (1991). Transcending the qualitative-quantitative debate: The analytic and systemic approaches to educational research. *Educational Researcher, 20,* 10-18.

Sandelowski, M., & Jones, L. C. (1995). "Healing fictions": Stories of choosing in the aftermath of the detection of fetal anomalies. *Social Science and Medicine, 42,* 353-361.

Sanjek, R. (1990). *Fieldnotes: The making of anthropology.* Albany: State University of New York Press.

Sarbin, T. R. (Ed.). (1986). *Narrative psychology: The storied nature of human conduct.* New York: Praeger.

Schafer, R. (1992). *Retelling a life: Narration and dialogue in psychoanalysis.* New York: Basic Books.

Schatzman, L., & Strauss, A. L. (1973). *Field research: Strategies for a natural sociology.* Englewood Cliffs, NJ: Prentice Hall.

Schein, E. H. (1987). *The clinical perspective in fieldwork.* Newbury Park, CA: Sage.

Schön, D. A. (1983). *The reflective practitioner: How professionals think in action.* New York: Basic Books.

Schwandt, T. A. (1994). Constructivist, interpretivist approaches to human inquiry. In N. K. Denzin & Y. S. Lincoln (Eds.), *Handbook of qualitative research* (pp. 118-137). Thousand Oaks, CA: Sage.

Schwandt, T. A., & Halpern, E. S. (1988). *Linking auditing and metaevaluation: Enhancing quality in applied research.* Newbury Park, CA: Sage.

Scriven, M. (1967). The methodology of evaluation. *AERA Monograph Series in Curriculum Evaluation, 1,* 39-83.

Sherman, E. (1994). Discourse analysis in the framework of change process research. In E. Sherman & W. J. Reid (Eds.), *Qualitative research in social work* (pp. 228-241). New York: Columbia University Press.

Sherman, E., & Reid, W. J. (Eds.). (1994). *Qualitative research in social work.* New York: Columbia University Press.

Siporin, M. (1988). Clinical social work as an art form. *Social Casework, 69,* 177-185.

Snow, D. A., & Anderson, L. (1991). Researching the homeless: The characteristic features and virtues of the case study. In J. R. Feagin, A. M. Orum, & G. Sjoberg (Eds.), *A case for the case study* (pp. 148-173). Chapel Hill: University of North Carolina Press.

Spence, D.P. (1982). *Narrative truth and historical truth: Meaning and interpretation in psychoanalysis.* New York: Norton.

Spradley, J. P. (1979). *The ethnographic interview.* New York: Holt, Rinehart & Winston.

Stack, C. B. (1974). *All our kin: Strategies for survival in a black community.* New York: Harper Colophon.

Stake, R. E. (1975). *Evaluating the arts in education: A responsive approach.* Columbus, OH: Merrill.

Stake, R. E. (1994). Case studies. In N. K. Denzin & Y. S. Lincoln (Eds.), *Handbook of qualitative research* (pp. 236-247). Thousand Oaks, CA: Sage.

Stange, K. C., Miller, W. L., Crabtree, B. F., O'Connor, P. J., & Zyzanski, S. J. (1994). Integrating qualitative and quantitative research methods. *Family Medicine, 21,* 448-451.

Stein, L. I., & Test, M. A. (1980). An alternative to mental hospital treatment I: Conceptual model, treatment program, and clinical evaluation. *Archives of General Psychiatry, 37,* 409-412.

Steinmetz, A. M. (1991). Doing. In M. Ely (with M. Anzul, T. Friedman, D. Garner, & A. M. Steinmetz), *Doing qualitative research: Circles within circles* (pp. 41-68). London: Falmer.

Stern, S. B. (1994). Commentary: Wanted! Social work practice evaluation and re-search—all methods considered. In E. Sherman & W. J. Reid (Eds.), *Qualitative research in social work* (pp. 485-492). New York: Columbia University Press.

Stiles, W. B. (1994). Views of the chasm between psychotherapy research and practice. In P. F. Talley, H. H. Strupp, & S. F. Butler (Eds.), *Psychotherapy research and practice* (pp. 154-166). New York: Basic Books.

Strauss, A., & Corbin, J. (1990). *Basics of qualitative research: Grounded theory procedures and techniques.* Newbury Park, CA: Sage.

Stringer, E. (1996). *Action research: A handbook for practitioners.* Thousand Oaks, CA: Sage.

Struening, E. L., Stueve, A., Vine, P., Kreisman, D. E., Link, B. G., & Herman, D. B. (1995). *Factors associated with grief and depressive symptoms in caregivers of people with serious mental illness.* New York: New York State Psychiatric Institute.

Susser, M. (1997). Authors and authorship: Reform or abolition? *American Journal of Public Health, 87,* 1091-1092.

Swigonski, M. E. (1994). The logic of feminist standpoint theory for social work research. *Social Work, 39,* 387-393.

Task Force on Social Work Research. (1991). *Building social work knowledge for effective services and policies: A plan for research development.* Washington, DC: Author.

Taylor, S. J. (1987). Observing abuse: Professional ethics and personal morality in field research. *Qualitative Sociology, 10,* 288-302.

Taylor, S. J., & Bogdan, R. (1980). Defending illusions: The institution's struggle for survival. *Human Organization, 39,* 209-218.

Taylor, S. J., & Bogdan, R. (1984). *Introduction to qualitative research: The search for meanings* (2nd ed.). New York: John Wiley.

Teller, V., & Dahl, H. (1986). The microstructure of free association. *Journal of the American Psychoanalytical Association, 34,* 763-798.

Tesch, R. (1990). *Qualitative research: Analysis types and software tools.* London: Falmer.

Tesch, R. (Ed.). (1991). Computers and qualitative data [Special issues, Parts 1 & 2]. *Qualitative Sociology, 13*(3 & 4).

Thyer, B. A. (1996). Forty years of progress toward empirical clinical practice? *Social Work Research, 20,* 77-81.

Tobin, S. S. (1994). Commentary: Narrative in clinical research. In E. Sherman & W. J. Reid (Eds.), *Qualitative research in social work* (pp. 200-204). New York: Columbia University Press.

Toseland, R. W. (1994). Commentary: The qualitative/quantitative debate: Moving beyond acrimony to meaningful dialogue. In E. Sherman & W. J. Reid (Eds.), *Qualitative research in social work* (pp. 453-458). New York: Columbia University Press.

Tsemberis, S. (1997). *Pathways to housing: An innovative model of supported housing for the homeless mentally ill in New York City.* New York: Pathways to Housing, Inc.

Tuchman, G. (1994). Historical social science: Methodologies, methods, and meanings. In N. K. Denzin & Y. S. Lincoln (Eds.), *Handbook of qualitative research* (pp. 306-323). Thousand Oaks, CA: Sage.

Tyson, K. (1994). Heuristic guidelines for naturalistic qualitative evaluations of child treatment. In E. Sherman & W. J. Reid (Eds.), *Qualitative research in social work* (pp. 89-114). New York: Columbia University Press.

Tyson, K. (1995). *New foundations for scientific social and behavioral research: The heuristic paradigm.* Boston: Allyn & Bacon.

Van Maanen, J. (1988). *Tales of the field: On writing ethnography.* Chicago: University of Chicago Press.

Videka-Sherman, L., & Reid, W. J. (1990). *Advances in clinical social work research.* Silver Spring, MD: NASW Press.

Vine, P. (1982). *Families in pain.* New York: Pantheon.

Walker, A. J., & Allen, K. R. (1991). Relationships between caregiving daughters and their elderly mothers. *The Gerontologist, 31,* 389-396.

Wax, R. H. (1971). *Doing fieldwork: Warnings and advice.* Chicago: University of Chicago Press.

Weinberg, D., & Koegel, P. (1996). Social model treatment and individuals with dual diagnoses: An ethnographic analysis of therapeutic practice. *The Journal of Mental Health Administration, 23,* 272-287.

Weiss, C. H. (1987). Where politics and evaluation research meet. In D. J. Palumbo (Ed.), *The politics of program evaluation* (pp. 47-70). Newbury Park, CA: Sage.

Weiss, R. S. (1994). *Learning from strangers: The art and method of qualitative interview studies.* New York: Free Press.

Whyte, W. F. (1955). *Street corner society* (2nd ed.). Chicago: University of Chicago Press.

Wolcott, H. F. (1988). Problem finding in qualitative research. In H. Trueba & C. Delgado-Gaitan (Eds.), *School and society: Learning content through culture* (pp. 11-35). New York: Praeger.

Wolcott, H. F. (1990). *Writing up qualitative research.* Newbury Park: CA: Sage.

Wolcott, H. F. (1994). *Transforming qualitative data.* Thousand Oaks, CA: Sage.

Wood, K. M. (1990). Epistemological issues in the development of social work practice knowledge. In L. Videka-Sherman & W. J. Reid (Eds.), *Advances in clinical social work research* (pp. 373-390). Washington, DC: NASW Press.

Workman, J. P., Jr. (1992). Use of electronic media in a participant observation study. *Qualitative Sociology, 15,* 419-425.

Yin, R. K. (1994). *Case study research: Design and methods.* Thousand Oaks, CA: Sage.

Zola, I. K. (1983). *Missing pieces: A chronicle of living with a disability.* Philadelphia: Temple University Press.

INDEX

ABOUT THE AUTHOR

DEBORAH K. PADGETT, PhD, is Associate Professor in the Research Area at the Ehrenkranz School of Social Work, New York University. She received her doctorate in anthropology in 1979 based on ethnographic research in a Serbian American community in Wisconsin and was a Fulbright research scholar in Zagreb, Croatia, in 1989. She completed postdoctoral fellowships in sociomedical sciences in 1986 at the Columbia University School of Public Health and in mental health services research in 1995 at Duke University, Department of Psychiatry. She has served on the Editorial Boards of *The Gerontologist* and *The Journal of Gerontology: Psychological and Social Sciences*, and on the Consulting Editorial Board of *Social Work*. She is also the editor of *The Handbook of Ethnicity, Aging, and Mental Health* (1995). She has published extensively on mental health needs and service use of the elderly, culturally diverse ethnic groups, the homeless, and children and adolescents. Her recent research interests are in women's health and mental health and in international studies of refugee/immigrant mental health. She is currently Co-Principal Investigator on a quantitative/qualitative study of African-American women and breast cancer screening in New York City.